THE TAVERN'S PLEASURES

Wine, Women, and Song

Students' Songs of the Middle Ages

John Addington Symonds

DOVER PUBLICATIONS, INC.
Mineola, New York

Published in Canada by General Publishing Company, Ltd., 895 Don Mills Road, 400-2 Park Centre, Toronto, Ontario M3C 1W3.

Published in the United Kingdom by David & Charles, Brunel House, Forde Close, Newton Abbot, Devon TQ12 4PU.

Bibliographical Note

Wine, Women, and Song was first published in 1884. This Dover edition, first published in 2002, is an unabridged republication of the 1907 edition published by Chatto & Windus, London, and The McClure Company, New York, as *Wine, Women, and Song: Medieval Latin Students' Songs Now First Translated Into English Verse With an Essay by John Addington Symonds.*

Library of Congress Cataloging-in-Publication Data

Carmina Burana. Selections. English.

Wine, women, and song : students' songs of the Middle Ages / [translated into English by] John Addington Symonds.

p. cm.

Originally published: London : Chatto & Windus, 1884.

Original ed. has subtitle: Mediæval Latin students' songs.

Largely composed of translations from Carmina Burana.

"Books on Goliardic literature": p.

ISBN 0-486-41913-4

1. Latin poetry, Medieval and modern–Translations into English. 2. Songs, Latin (Medieval and modern)–Translations into English. 3. Goliards–Songs and music–Texts. 4. Students' songs.–Texts. I. Symonds, John Addington, 1840–1893. II. Title.

PA8164 .C37 2002

874'.0308–dc21

2001032322

Manufactured in the United States of America
Dover Publications, Inc., 31 East 2nd Street, Mineola, N.Y. 11501

" WER LIEBT NICHT WEIB WEIN UND GESANG

DER BLEIBT EIN NARR SEIN LEBENSLANG."

Martin Luther.

CONTENTS

CONTENTS

LIST OF ILLUSTRATIONS

The above six woodcuts are reproduced from the "Navis Stultifera" of Sebastian Brandt, first Latin edition, 1497.

WINE, WOMEN, AND SONG

I

WHEN we try to picture to ourselves the intellectual and moral state of Europe in the
Middle Ages, some fixed and almost stereotyped ideas
immediately suggest themselves. We think of the
nations immersed in a gross mental lethargy; passively
witnessing the gradual extinction of arts and sciences
which Greece and Rome had splendidly inaugurated;
allowing libraries and monuments of antique civilisation
to crumble into dust; while they trembled under a dull
and brooding terror of coming judgment, shrank from
natural enjoyment as from deadly sin, or yielded themselves with brutal eagerness to the satisfaction of vulgar
appetites. Preoccupation with the other world in this
long period weakens man's hold upon the things that
make his life desirable. Philosophy is sunk in the
slough of ignorant, perversely subtle disputation upon
subjects destitute of actuality. Theological fanaticism
has extinguished liberal studies and the gropings of the
reason after truth in positive experience. Society lies
prostrate under the heel of tyrannous orthodoxy. We
discern men in masses, aggregations, classes, guilds—
everywhere the genus and the species of humanity,
rarely and by luminous exception individuals and

persons. Universal ideals of Church and Empire clog and confuse the nascent nationalities. Prolonged habits of extra-mundane contemplation, combined with the decay of real knowledge, volatilise the thoughts and aspirations of the best and wisest into dreamy un-realities, giving a false air of mysticism to love, shroud-ing art in allegory, reducing the interpretation of texts to an exercise of idle ingenuity, and the study of Nature (in Bestiaries, Lapidaries, and the like) to an insane system of grotesque and pious quibbling. The conception of man's fall and of the incurable badness of this world bears poisonous fruit of cynicism and asceticism, that twofold bitter almond hidden in the harsh monastic shell. The devil has become God upon this earth, and God's eternal jailer in the next world. Nature is regarded with suspicion and aver-sion; the flesh, with shame and loathing, broken by spasmodic outbursts of lawless self-indulgence. For human life there is one formula :—

> " Of what is't fools make such vain keeping ?
>   Sin their conception, their birth weeping,
>   Their life a general mist of error,
>   Their death a hideous storm of terror."

The contempt of the world is the chief theme of edification. A charnel filled with festering corpses, snakes, and worms points the preacher's moral. Before the eyes of all, in terror-stricken vision or in nightmares of uneasy conscience, leap the inextinguish-able flames of hell. Salvation, meanwhile, is being sought through amulets, relics, pilgrimages to holy places, fetishes of divers sorts and different degrees of potency. The faculties of the heart and head, defrauded of wholesome sustenance, have recourse to delirious debauches of the fancy, dreams of magic, compacts with the evil one, insanities of desire, ineptitudes of discipline. Sexual passion, ignoring the true place of woman in society, treats her on the one hand like a servile instrument, on the other exalts her to sainthood or execrates her as the chief impediment to holiness. Common sense, sanity of judgment, acceptance of things as they are, resolution to ameliorate the evils and to utilise the goods of life, seem everywhere deficient. Men are obstinate in misconception of their proper aims, wasting their energies upon shadows instead of holding fast by realities, waiting for a future whereof they know nothing, in lieu of mastering and economising the present. The largest and most serious undertakings of united Europe in this period—the Crusades —are based upon a radical mistake. "Why seek ye the living among the dead? Behold, He is not here, but risen!" With these words ringing in their ears, the nations flock to Palestine and pour their blood forth for an empty sepulchre. The one Emperor who attains the object of Christendom by rational means is excommunicated for his success. Frederick II. returns from the Holy Land a ruined man because he made a compact useful to his Christian subjects with the Chief of Islam.

II

Such are some of the stereotyped ideas which crowd our mind when we reflect upon the Middle Ages. They are certainly one-sided. Drawn for the most part from the study of monastic literature, exaggerated by that reaction against medievalism which the Renaissance initiated, they must be regarded as inadequate to represent the whole truth. At no one period between the fall of the Roman Empire and the close of the thirteenth century was the mental atmosphere of Europe so unnaturally clouded. Yet there is sufficient substance in them to justify their formulation. The earlier Middle Ages did, in fact, extinguish antique civility. The later Middle Ages did create, to use a phrase of Michelet, an army of dunces for the maintenance of orthodoxy. The intellect and the conscience became used to moving paralytically among visions, dreams, and mystic terrors, weighed down with torpor, abusing virile faculties for the suppression of truth and the perpetuation of revered error.

It is, therefore, with a sense of surprise, with something like a shock to preconceived opinions, that we first become acquainted with the medieval literature which it is my object in the present treatise to make better known to English readers. That so bold, so fresh, so natural, so pagan a view of human life as the Latin songs of the Wandering Students exhibit, should have found clear and artistic utterance in the epoch of the Crusades, is indeed enough to bid us pause and reconsider the justice of our stereotyped ideas about that period. This literature makes it manifest that the ineradicable appetites and natural instincts of men and women were no less vigorous in fact, though less articulate and self-assertive, than they had been in the age of Greece and Rome, and than they afterwards displayed themselves in what is known as the Renaissance.

With something of the same kind we have long been familiar in the Troubadour poetry of Provence. But Provençal literature has a strong chivalrous tincture, and every one is aware with what relentless fury the civilisation which produced it was stamped out by the Church. The literature of the Wandering Students, on the other hand, owes nothing to chivalry, and emanates from a class which formed a subordinate part of the ecclesiastical militia. It is almost vulgar in its presentment of common human impulses; it bears the mark of the proletariate, though adorned with flourishes betokening the neighbourhood of Church and University.

III

Much has recently been written upon the subject of an abortive Renaissance within the Middle Ages. The centre of it was France, and its period of brilliancy may be roughly defined as the middle and end of the twelfth century. Much, again, has been said about the religious movement in England, which spread to Eastern Europe, and anticipated the Reformation by two centuries before the date of Luther. The songs of the Wandering Students, composed for the most part in the twelfth century, illustrate both of these early efforts after self-emancipation. Uttering the unrestrained emotions of men attached by a slender tie to the dominant clerical class and diffused over all countries, they bring us face to face with a body of opinion which finds in studied chronicle or laboured dissertation of the period no echo. On the one side, they express that delight in life and physical enjoyment which was a main characteristic of the Renaissance ; on the other, they proclaim that revolt against the corruption of Papal Rome which was the motive-force of the Reformation.

Our knowledge of this poetry is derived from two chief sources. One is a MS. of the thirteenth century, which was long preserved in the monastery of Benedict-beuern in Upper Bavaria, and is now at Munich. Richly illuminated with rare and curious illustrations of contemporary manners, it seems to have been compiled for the use of some ecclesiastical prince. This fine codex was edited in 1847 at Stuttgart. The title of the publication is *Carmina Burana,* and under that designation I shall refer to it. The other is a Harleian MS., written before 1264, which Mr. Thomas Wright collated with other English MSS., and published in 1841 under the name of *Latin Poems commonly attributed to Walter Mapes.*

These two sources have to some extent a common stock of poems, which proves the wide diffusion of the songs in question before the date assignable to the earlier of the two MS. authorities. But while this is so, it must be observed that the *Carmina Burana* are richer in compositions which form a prelude to the Renaissance; the English collections, on the other hand, contain a larger number of serious and satirical pieces anticipating the Reformation.

Another important set of documents for the study of the subject are the three large works of Edelstand du Méril upon popular Latin poetry; while the stores at our disposal have been otherwise augmented by occasional publications of German and English scholars, bringing to light numerous scattered specimens of a like description. Of late it has been the fashion in Germany to multiply anthologies of medieval student-songs, intended for companion volumes to the *Commersbuch*. Among these, one entitled *Gaudeamus* (Teubner, 2d edition, 1879) deserves honourable mention.

It is my purpose to give a short account of what is known about the authors of these verses, to analyse the general characteristics of their art, and to illustrate the theme by copious translations. So far as I am aware, the songs of Wandering Students offer almost absolutely untrodden ground to the English translator; and this fact may be pleaded in excuse for the large number which I have laid under contribution.

In carrying out my plan, I shall confine myself principally, but not strictly, to the *Carmina Burana*. I wish to keep in view the anticipation of the Renaissance rather than to dwell upon those elements which indicate an early desire for ecclesiastical reform.

IV

We have reason to conjecture that the Romans, even during the classical period of their literature, used accentual rhythms for popular poetry, while quantitative metres formed upon Greek models were the artificial modes employed by cultivated writers. However this may be, there is no doubt that, together with the decline of antique civilisation, accent and rhythm began to displace quantity and metre in Latin versification. Quantitative measures, like the Sapphic and Hexameter, were composed accentually. The services and music of the Church introduced new systems of prosody. Rhymes, both single and double, were added to the verse; and the extraordinary flexibility of medieval Latin—that sonorous instrument of varied rhetoric used by Augustine in the prose of the *Confessions,* and gifted with poetic inspiration in such hymns as the *Dies Irae* or the *Stabat Mater*—rendered this new vehicle of literary utterance adequate to all the tasks imposed on it by piety and metaphysic. The language of the *Confessions* and the *Dies Irae* is not, in fact, a decadent form of Cicero's prose or Virgil's verse, but a development of the Roman speech in accordance with the new conditions introduced by Christianity. It remained comparatively sterile in the department of prose composition, but it attained to high qualities of art in the verse and rhythms of men like Thomas of Celano, Thomas of Aquino, Adam of St. Victor, Bernard of Morlais, and Bernard of Clairvaux.

At the same time, classical Latin literature continued to be languidly studied in the cloisters and the schools of grammar. The metres of the ancients were practised with uncouth and patient assiduity, strenuous efforts being made to keep alive an art which was no longer rightly understood. Rhyme invaded the hexameter, and the best verses of the medieval period in that measure were leonine.

The hymns of the Church and the secular songs composed for music in this base Latin took a great variety of rhythmic forms. It is clear that vocal melody controlled their movement; and one fixed element in all these compositions was rhyme—rhyme often intricate and complex beyond hope of imitation in our language. Elision came to be disregarded; and even the accentual values, which may at first have formed a substitute for quantity, yielded to musical notation. The epithet of popular belongs to these songs in a very real sense, since they were intended for the people's use, and sprang from popular emotion. Poems of this class were technically known as *moduli*— a name which points significantly to the importance of music in their structure. Imitations of Ovid's elegiacs or of Virgil's hexameters obtained the name of *versus*. Thus Walter of Lille, the author of a regular epic poem on Alexander, one of the best medieval writers of *versus*, celebrates his skill in the other department of popular poetry thus—

"Perstrepuit *modulis* Gallia tota meis."
(All France rang with my songs.)

We might compare the *versus* of the Middle Ages

with the stiff sculptures on a Romanesque font, life-
lessly reminiscent of decadent classical art; while the
moduli, in their freshness, elasticity, and vigour of
invention, resemble the floral scrolls, foliated cusps,
and grotesque basreliefs of Gothic or Lombard
architecture.

V

Even in the half-light of what used to be called
emphatically the Dark Ages, there pierce gleams
which may be reflections from the past evening of
paganism, or may intimate the earliest dawn of
modern times. One of these is a song, partly popular,
partly scholastic, addressed to a beautiful boy.[1] It
begins thus—

"O admirabile veneris idŏlum"—

and continues in this strain, upon the same rhythm,
blending reminiscences of classical mythology and
medieval metaphysic, and winding up with a reference
to the Horatian *Vitas hinnuleo me similis Chloe*. This
poem was composed in the seventh century, probably
at Verona, for mention is made in it of the river
Adige. The metre can perhaps be regarded as a
barbarous treatment of the long Asclepiad; but each
line seems to work out into two bars, divided by a
marked rest, with two accents to each bar, and shows

[1] Du Méril, *Poésies Populaires Latines Antérieures au Deuxième
Siècle*, p. 240.

by what sort of transition the modern French Alexandrine may have been developed.

The oddly archaic phraseology of this love-song
rendered it unfit for translation ; but I have tried my
hand at a kind of hymn in praise of Rome, which is
written in the same peculiar rhythm : [1] —

"O Rome illustrious, of the world emperess!
Over all cities thou queen in thy goodliness!
Red with the roseate blood of the martyrs, and
White with the lilies of virgins at God's right hand !
Welcome we sing to thee; ever we bring to thee
Blessings, and pay to thee praise for eternity.

Peter, thou praepotent warder of Paradise,
Hear thou with mildness the prayer of thy votaries;
When thou art seated to judge the twelve tribes, O then
Show thyself merciful ; be thou benign to men;
And when we call to thee now in the world's distress,
Take thou our suffrages, master, with gentleness.

Paul, to our litanies lend an indulgent ear,
Who the philosophers vanquished with zeal severe :
Thou that art steward now in the Lord's heavenly
   house,
Give us to taste of the meat of grace bounteous ;
So that the wisdom which filled thee and nourished thee
May be our sustenance through the truths taught by thee."

A curious secular piece of the tenth century deserves
more than passing mention. It shows how wine,
women, and song, even in an age which is supposed to
have trembled for the coming destruction of the world,
still formed the attraction of some natures.   What is
more, there is a certain modern, as distinguished from

---

[1] Du Méril, *op. cit.*, p. 239.

classical, tone of tenderness in the sentiment.   It is
the invitation of a young man to his mistress, bidding
her to a little supper in his rooms : [1] —

> " Come therefore now, my gentle fere,
>   Whom as my heart I hold full dear ;
>   Enter my little room, which is
>   Adorned with quaintest rarities :
>   There are the seats with cushions spread,
>   The roof with curtains overhead ;
>   The house with flowers of sweetest scent
>   And scattered herbs is redolent :
>   A table there is deftly dight
>   With meats and drinks of rare delight ;
>   There too the wine flows, sparkling, free ;
>   And all, my love, to pleasure thee.
>   There sound enchanting symphonies ;
>   The clear high notes of flutes arise ;
>   A singing girl and artful boy
>   Are chanting for thee strains of joy ;
>   He touches with his quill the wire,
>   She tunes her note unto the lyre :
>   The servants carry to and fro
>   Dishes and cups of ruddy glow ;
>   But these delights, I will confess,
>   Than pleasant converse charm me less ;
>   Nor is the feast so sweet to me
>   As dear familiarity.
>   Then come now, sister of my heart,
>   That dearer than all others art,
>   Unto mine eyes thou shining sun,
>   Soul of my soul, thou only one !
>   I dwelt alone in the wild woods,
>   And loved all secret solitudes ;
>   Oft would I fly from tumults far,
>   And shunned where crowds of people are.

---

[1] Du Méril, *Poésies Populaires Latines du Moyen Age*, p. 196.

O dearest, do not longer stay !
Seek we to live and love to-day !
I cannot live without thee, sweet !
Time bids us now our love complete.
Why should we then defer, my own,
What must be done or late or soon ?
Do quickly what thou canst not shun !
I have no hesitation."

From Du Méril's collections further specimens of
thoroughly secular poetry might be culled.   Such is
the panegyric of the nightingale, which contains the
following impassioned lines : [1]—

"Implet silvas atque cuncta modulis arbustula,
    Gloriosa valde facta veris prae laetitia ;
    Volitando scandit alta arborum cacumina,
    Ac festiva satis gliscit sibilare carmina."

Such are the sapphics on the spring, which, though
they date from the seventh century, have a truly modern
sentiment of Nature.   Such, too, is the medieval
legend of the Snow-Child, treated comically in burlesque Latin verse, and meant to be sung to a German
tune of love—*Modus Liebinc*.   To the same category
may be referred the horrible, but singularly striking,
series of Latin poems edited from a MS. at Berne,
which set forth the miseries of monastic life with
realistic passion bordering upon delirium, under titles
like the following—*Dissuasio Concubitûs in Uno tantum
Sexu*, or *De Monachi Cruciatu*.[2]

---

[1] Du Méril, *Poésies Pop. Lat. Ant.*, pp. 278, 241, 275.

[2] These extraordinary compositions will be found on pp.
174–182 of a closely-printed book entitled *Carmina Med.
Aev. Max. Part. Inedita.   Ed. H. Hagenus.   Bernae.   Ap.
G. Frobenium.*   MDCCCLXXVII.   The editor, so far as I can

VI

There is little need to dwell upon these crepuscular
stirrings of popular Latin poetry in the earlier Middle
Ages. To indicate their existence was necessary ; for
they serve to link by a dim and fragile thread of evolution the decadent art of the base Empire with the
renascence of paganism attempted in the twelfth century,
and thus to connect that dawn of modern feeling with
the orient splendours of the fourteenth and fifteenth
centuries in Italy.

The first point to notice is the dominance of music
in this verse, and the subjugation of the classic metres
to its influence. A deeply significant transition has
been effected from the *versus* to the *modulus* by the
substitution of accent for quantity, and by the value
given to purely melodic cadences. A long syllable and
a short syllable have almost equal weight in this prosody, for the musical tone can be prolonged or shortened
upon either. So now the *cantilena*, rather than the *metron*,
rules the flow of verse ; but, at the same time, antique
forms are still conventionally used, though violated in
the using. In other words, the modern metres of the
modern European races—the Italian Hendecasyllable,
the French Alexandrine, the English Iambic and

---

discover, gives but scant indication of the poet who lurks,
with so much style and so terrible emotions, under the veil
of Cod. Bern., 702 s. Any student who desires to cut into
the core of cloister life should read cvii. pp. 178–182, of this
little book.

Trochaic rhythms—have been indicated ; and a moment has been prepared when these measures shall tune themselves by means of emphasis and accent to song, before they take their place as literary schemes appealing to the ear in rhetoric.   This phase, whereby the metres of antiquity pass into the rhythms of the modern races, implies the use of medieval Latin, still not unmindful of classic art, but governed now by music often of Teutonic origin, and further modified by affinities of prosody imported from Teutonic sources.

The next point to note is that, in this process of transition, popular ecclesiastical poetry takes precedence of secular.   The great rhyming structures of the Middle Ages, which exercised so wide an influence over early European literature, were invented for the service of the Church—voluminous systems of recurrent double rhymes, intricate rhythms moulded upon tunes for chanting, solid melodic fabrics, which, having once been formed, were used for lighter efforts of the fancy, or lent their ponderous effects to parody.   Thus, in the first half of the centuries which intervene between the extinction of the genuine Roman Empire and the year 1300, ecclesiastical poetry took the lead in creating and popularising new established types of verse, and in rendering the spoken Latin pliable for various purposes of art.

A third point worthy of attention is, that a certain breath of paganism, wafting perfumes from the old mythology, whispering of gods in exile, encouraging men to accept their life on earth with genial enjoyment, was never wholly absent during the darkest periods of

the Middle Ages.   This inspiration uttered itself in
Latin ; for we have little reason to believe that the
modern languages had yet attained plasticity enough for
the expression of that specific note which belongs to
the Renaissance—the note of humanity conscious of
its Græco-Roman pagan past.   This Latin, meanwhile, which it employed was fabricated by the Church
and used by men of learning.

VII

The songs of the Wandering Students were in a strict
sense *moduli* as distinguished from *versus ;* popular and
not scholastic.   They were, however, composed by
men of culture, imbued with classical learning of some
sort, and prepared by scholarship for the deftest and
most delicate manipulation of the Latin language.

Who were these Wandering Students, so often mentioned, and of whom nothing has been as yet related ?
As their name implies, they were men, and for the most
part young men, travelling from university to university
in search of knowledge.   Far from their homes, without responsibilities, light of purse and light of heart,
careless and pleasure-seeking, they ran a free, disreput-
able course, frequenting taverns at least as much as
lecture-rooms, more capable of pronouncing judgment upon wine or women than upon a problem of
divinity or logic.   The conditions of medieval learning
made it necessary to study different sciences in different
parts of Europe ; and a fixed habit of unrest, which

seems to have pervaded society after the period of the Crusades, encouraged vagabondage in all classes. The extent to which travelling was carried in the Middle Ages for purposes of pilgrimage and commerce, out of pure curiosity or love of knowledge, for the bettering of trade in handicrafts or for self-improvement in the sciences, has only of late years been estimated at a just calculation. "The scholars," wrote a monk of Froidmont in the twelfth century, "are wont to roam around the world and visit all its cities, till much learning makes them mad; for in Paris they seek liberal arts, in Orleans authors, at Salerno gallipots, at Toledo demons, and in no place decent manners."

These pilgrims to the shrines of knowledge formed a class apart. They were distinguished from the secular and religious clergy, inasmuch as they had taken no orders, or only minor orders, held no benefice or cure, and had entered into no conventual community. They were still more sharply distinguished from the laity, whom they scorned as brutes, and with whom they seem to have lived on terms of mutual hostility. One of these vagabond gownsmen would scarcely condescend to drink with a townsman: [1]—

> "In aeterno igni
> Cruciantur rustici, qui non sunt tam digni
> Quod bibisse noverint bonum vinum vini."

> "Aestimetur laicus ut brutus,
> Nam ad artem surdus est et mutus."

[1] See the drinking song printed in *Walter Mapes*, p. xlv., and *Carm. Bur.*, pp. 198, 179.

"Litteratos convocat decus virginale,
Laicorum execrat pectus bestiale."

In a parody of the Mass, which is called *Officium Lusorum*, and in which the prayers are offered to Bacchus, we find this devout collect : [1]—"Omnipotens sempiterne deus, qui inter rusticos et clericos magnam discordiam seminasti, praesta quaesumus de laboribus eorum vivere, de mulieribus ipsorum vero et de morte deciorum semper gaudere."

The English version of this ribald prayer is even more explicit. It runs thus :—"Deus qui multitudinem rusticorum ad servitium clericorum venire fecisti et militum et inter nos et ipsos discordiam seminasti."

It is open to doubt whether the *milites* or soldiers were included with the rustics in that laity, for which the students felt so bitter a contempt. But the tenor of some poems on love, especially the *Dispute of Phyllis and Flora*, shows that the student claimed a certain superiority over the soldier. This antagonism between clerk and rustic was heartily reciprocated. In a song on taverns the student is warned that he may meet with rough treatment from the clodhopper : [2]—

"O clerici dilecti,
Discite vitare
Tabernam horribilem,
Qui cupitis regnare;

---

[1] *Carm. Bur.*, p. 249, note. There is a variation in the parody printed by Wright, *Rel. Antiq.*, ii.

[2] See A. P. von Bärnstein's little volume, *Ubi sunt qui ante nos*, p. 46.

> Nec audeant vos rustici
>   Plagis verberare!
> Rusticus dum se
>   Sentit ebriatum,
> Clericum non reputat
>   Militem armatum.
> Vere plane consulo
>   Ut abstineatis,
> Nec unquam cum rusticis
>   Tabernam ineatis."

The affinities of the Wandering Students were rather
with the Church than with laymen of any degree.
They piqued themselves upon their title of *Clerici*, and
added the epithet of *Vagi*.   We shall see in the sequel
that they stood in a peculiar relation of dependence
upon ecclesiastical society.

According to tendencies prevalent in the Middle Ages,
they became a sort of guild, and proclaimed themselves with pride an Order.   Nothing is more clearly
marked in their poetry than the *esprit de corps*, which
animates them with a cordial sense of brotherhood.[1]
The same tendencies which prompted their association
required that they should have a patron saint.   But
as the confraternity was anything but religious, this
saint, or rather this eponymous hero, had to be a
Rabelaisian character.   He was called Golias, and
his flock received the generic name of Goliardi.
Golias was father and master; the Goliardi were his
family, his sons, and pupils.   *Familia Goliae, Magister
Golias, Pueri Goliae, Discipulus Goliae,* are phrases to
be culled from the rubrics of their literature.

[1] See especially the songs *Ordo Noster* and *Nos Vagabunduli*,
translated below in Section xiii.

Much has been conjectured regarding these names and titles. Was Golias a real person? Did he give his own name to the Goliardi; or was he invented after the Goliardi had already acquired their designation? In either case, ought we to connect both words with the Latin *gula*, and so regard the Goliardi as notable gluttons; or with the Provençal *goliar, gualiar, gualiardor*, which carry a significance of deceit? Had Golias anything to do with Goliath of the Bible, the great Philistine, who in the present day would more properly be chosen as the hero of those classes which the students held in horror?

It is not easy to answer these questions. All we know for certain is, that the term Goliardus was in common medieval use, and was employed as a synonym for Wandering Scholar in ecclesiastical documents. *Vagi scholares aut Goliardi—joculatores, goliardi seu bufones—goliardia vel histrionatus—vagi scholares qui goliardi vel histriones alio nomine appellantur—clerici ribaudi, maxime qui dicuntur de familia Goliae :* so run the acts of several Church Councils.[1] The word passed into modern languages. The *Grandes Chroniques de S. Denis* speak of *jugleor, enchanteor, goliardois, et autres manières de menestrieux*. Chaucer, in his description of the Miller, calls this merry narrator of fabliaux *a jangler and a goliardeis*. In *Piers Ploughman* the *goliardeis* is further explained to be *a glutton of words*, and talks in Latin rhyme.[2]

Giraldus Cambrensis, during whose lifetime the

[1] See Wright's introduction to *Walter Mapes*.
[2] Ibid.

name Golias first came into vogue, thought that this
father of the Goliardic family was a real person.[1]   He
writes of him thus :—" A certain parasite called Golias,
who in our time obtained wide notoriety for his gluttony
and lechery, and by addiction to gulosity and debauchery
deserved his surname, being of excellent culture but of
bad manners, and of no moral discipline, uttered oftentimes and in many forms, both of rhythm and metre,
infamous libels against the Pope and Curia of Rome,
with no less impudence than imprudence." This is
perhaps the most outspoken utterance with regard to
the eponymous hero of the Goliardic class which we
possess, and it deserves a close inspection.

In the first place, Giraldus attributes the satiric poems
which passed under the name of Golias to a single
author famous in his days, and says of this poet that he
used both modern rhythms and classical metres.   The
description would apply to Gualtherus de Insula, Walter
of Lille, or, as he is also called, Walter of Chatillon ;
for some of this Walter's satires are composed in a
curious mixture of the rhyming measures of the
medieval hymns with classical hexameters.[2]   Yet had
Giraldus been pointing at Walter of Lille, a notable
personage in his times, there is no good reason to suppose that he would have suppressed his real name, or
have taken for granted that Golias was a *bona fide* surname.   On the theory that he knew Golias to be a

---

[1] See Wright's introduction to *Walter Mapes*.

[2] See Müldner, *Die zehn Gedichte des Walther von Lille*,
1859. Walter Mapes (ed. Wright) is credited with five of
these satires, including two which close each stanza with a
hexameter from Juvenal, Virgil, Ovid, Lucan, Horace.

mere nickname, and was aware that Walter of Lille
was the actual satirist, we should have to explain his
paragraph by the hypothesis that he chose to sneer at
him under his *nom de guerre* instead of stigmatising him
openly in person.

His remarks, at any rate, go far toward disposing of
the old belief that the Goliardic satires were the work
of Thomas Mapes. Giraldus was an intimate friend
of that worthy, who deserves well of all lovers of
medieval romance as a principal contributor to the
Arthurian cycle. It is hardly possible that Giraldus
should have gibbeted such a man under the sobriquet
of Golias.

But what, it may be asked, if Walter of Lille, without the cognisance of our English annalist, had in
France obtained the chief fame of these poems? what
if they afterwards were attributed in England to
another Walter, his contemporary, himself a satirist of
the monastic orders? The fact that Walter of Lille
was known in Latin as Gualtherus de Insula, or
Walter of the Island, may have confirmed the mis-
apprehension thus suggested. It should be added that
the ascription of the Goliardic satires to Walter Mapes
or Map first occurs in MSS. of the fourteenth century.

VIII

I do not think there is much probability of arriving
at certainty with regard to the problems indicated in

the foregoing section.   We must be content to accept
the names Golias and Goliardi as we find them, and
to treat of this literature as the product of a class, from
the midst of which, as it is clear to any critic, more
than one poet rose to eminence.

One thing appears manifest from the references to
the Goliardi which I have already quoted.   That is,
that the Wandering Students ranked in common esti-
mation with jongleurs, buffoons, and minstrels.   Both
classes held a similar place in medieval society.   Both
were parasites devoted to the entertainment of their
superiors in rank.   Both were unattached, except by
occasional engagements, to any fixed abode.   But
while the minstrels found their temporary homes in the
castles of the nobility, we have reason to believe that
the Goliardi haunted abbeys and amused the leisure of
ecclesiastical lords.

The personality of the writer disappears in nearly all
the *Carmina Vagorum.*   Instead of a poet with a name,
we find a type ; and the verse is put into the mouth of
Golias himself, or the Archipoeta, or the Primate of
the order.   This merging of the individual in the class
of which he forms a part is eminently characteristic of
popular literature, and separates the Goliardic songs
from those of the Provençal Troubadours.   The
emotions to which popular poetry gives expression are
generic rather than personal.   They are such that all
the world, granted common sympathies and common
proclivities, can feel them and adopt the mode of
utterance invented for them by the singer.   If there
be any bar to their universal acceptance, it is only such

as may belong to the peculiar conditions of the social class from which they have emanated. The *Rispetti* of Tuscany imply a certain form of peasant life. The *Carmina Vagorum* are coloured to some extent by the prejudices and proclivities of vagabond existence.

Trenchantly true as the inspiration of a popular lyric may be, inevitable as may be the justice of its sentiment, unerring as may be its touch upon reality, still it lacks the note which marks it out for one man's utterance among a thousand. Composing it, the one has made himself the mouthpiece of the thousand. What the *Volkslied* gains in universality it loses in individuality of character. Its applicability to human nature at large is obtained at the sacrifice of that interest which belongs to special circumstances. It suits every one who grieves or loves or triumphs. It does not indicate the love, the grief, the triumph of this man and no other. It possesses the pathos and the beauty ot countless human lives prolonged through inarticulate generations, finding utterance at last in it. It is deficient in that particular intonation which makes a Shelley's voice differ from a Leopardi's, Petrarch's sonnets for Laura differ from Sidney's sonnets for Stella. It has always less of perceptible artistic effect, more enduring human quality. Some few of its lines are so well found, so rightly said, that they possess the certainty of natural things—a quality rare in the works of all but the greatest known poets. But these phrases with the accent of truest truth are often embedded in mere generalities and repetitions.

These characteristics of popular poetry help to

explain the frequent recurrence of the same ideas, the same expressions, the same stanzas even, in the lyrics of the Goliardi. A *Volkslied,* once created, becomes common property. It flies abroad like thistledown; settles and sows its seed; is maimed and mutilated; is improved or altered for the worse; is curtailed, expanded, adapted to divers purposes at different times and in very different relations.

We may dismiss the problem of authorship partly as insoluble, partly as of slight importance for a literature which is manifestly popular. With even greater brevity may the problem of nationality be disposed of. Some critics have claimed an Italian, some an English, some a French, and some a German origin for the *Carmina Vagorum.* The truth is that, just as the *Clerici Vagi* were themselves of all nations, so were their songs; and the use of a Latin common to all Europe in the Middle Ages renders it difficult even to conjecture the soil from which any particular lyric may have sprung. As is natural, a German codex contains more songs of Teutonic origin; an English displays greater abundance of English compositions. I have already observed that our two chief sources of Goliardic literature have many elements in common; but the treasures of the Benedictbeuern MS. differ in complexion from those of the Harleian in important minor details; and it is probable that if French and Italian stores were properly ransacked—which has not yet been done—we should note in them similar characteristic divergences.

The *Carmina Burana,* by their frequent references to

linden-trees and nightingales, and their numerous German refrains, indicate a German home for the poems on
spring and love, in which they are specially rich.[1]
The collections of our own land have an English turn
of political thought; the names Anglia and Anglus not
unfrequently occur; and the use of the word " Schel-
linck " in one of the *Carmina Burana* may point, perhaps, to an English origin.   France claims her own,
not only in the acknowledged pieces of Walter de
Lille, but also in a few which exhibit old French
refrains.   To Italian conditions, if not to Italian poets,
we may refer those that introduce spreading pines or
olive-trees into their pictures, and one which yields the
refrain *Bela mia.*   The most important lyric of the
series, *Golias' Confession,* was undoubtedly written at
Pavia, but whether by an Italian or not we do not
know.   The probability is rather, perhaps, in favour of
Teutonic authorship, since this *Confession* is addressed
to a German prelate.   Here it may be noticed that
the proper names of places and people are frequently
altered to suit different countries; while in some cases
they are indicated by an N, sufficiently suggestive of
their generality.   Thus the *Confession of Golias* in the
Carmina Burana mentions *Electe Coloniae ;* in an English
version, introduces *Praesul Coventriae.*   The prayer
for alms, which I have translated in Section xiii., is
addressed to *Decus N—,* thou honour of Norwich

---

[1] The more I study the songs of love and wine in this
codex, the more convinced am I that they have their origin
for the most part in South-Western Germany, Bavaria, the
Bodensee, and Elsass.

town, or Wittenberg, or wherever the wandering
scholar may have chanced to be.

With regard to the form and diction of the *Carmina
Vagorum*, it is enough to say two things at the present
time. First, a large portion of these pieces, including
a majority of the satires and longer descriptive poems,
are composed in measures borrowed from hymnology,
follow the diction of the Church, and imitate the
double-rhyming rhythms of her sequences. It is not
unnatural, this being the case, that parodies of hymns
should be comparatively common. Of these I shall
produce some specimens in the course of this study.
Secondly, those which do not exhibit popular hymn
measures are clearly written for melodies, some of
them very complicated in structure, suggesting part-
songs and madrigals, with curious interlacing of long
and short lines, double and single rhymes, recurrent
ritournelles, and so forth.

The ingenuity with which these poets adapted their
language to the exigencies of the tune, taxing the
fertility of Latin rhymes, and setting off the long
sonorous words to great advantage, deserves admiring
comment. At their best, it is almost impossible to
reproduce in English the peculiar effects of their
melodic artifices. But there is another side to the
matter. At their worst, these Latin lyrics, moulded
on a tune, degenerate into disjointed verbiage, sound
and adaptation to song prevailing over sense and satisfaction to the mind. It must, however, be remembered
that such lyrics, sometimes now almost unintelligible,
have come down to us with a very mutilated text

after suffering the degradations through frequent oral transmission to which popular poetry is peculiarly liable.

IX

It is easier to say what the Goliardi wrote about than who the writers were, and what they felt and thought than by what names they were baptised. The mass of their literature, as it is at present known to us, divides into two broad classes. The one division includes poems on the themes of vagabond existence, the truant life of these capricious students; on springtime and its rural pleasure; on love in many phases and for divers kinds of women; lastly, on wine and on the dice-box. The other division is devoted to graver topics; to satires on society, touching especially the Roman Court, and criticising eminent ecclesiastics in all countries; to moral dissertations, and to discourses on the brevity of life.

Of the two divisions, the former yields by far the livelier image of the men we have to deal with. It will therefore form the staple of my argument. The latter blends at so many points with medieval literature of the monastic kind, that it is chiefly distinguished by boldness of censure and sincerity of invective. In these qualities the serious poems of the Goliardi, emanating from a class of men who moved behind the scenes and yet were free to speak their thoughts, are unique. Written with the satirist's eye upon the object of his sarcasm, tinged with the license of his vagabondage, throbbing with the passionate and nonchalant afflatus of the wine-cup, they wing their flight like poisoned arrows or plumed serpents with unerring straightness at abuses in high places.

The wide space occupied by Nature in the secular poems of the Goliardi is remarkable. As a background to their love-songs we always find the woods and fields of May, abundant flowers and gushing rivulets, lime-trees and pines and olive-trees, through which soft winds are blowing. There are rose-bowers and nightingales; fauns, nymphs, and satyrs dancing on the sward. Choirs of mortal maidens emerge in the midst of this Claude-landscape. The scene, meanwhile, has been painted from experience, and felt with the enthusiasm of affection. It breathes of healthy open air, of life upon the road, of casual joys and wayside pleasure, snatched with careless heart by men whose tastes are natural. There is very little of the alcove or the closet in this verse; and the touch upon the world is so infantine, so tender, that we are indulgent to the generalities with which the poets deal.

What has been said about popular poetry applies also to popular painting. In the landscapes of Goliardic literature there is nothing specific to a single locality—no name like Vaucluse, no pregnant touch that indicates one scene selected from a thousand. The landscape is always a background, more northern or more southern as the case may be, but penetrated with the feeling of the man who has been happy or has suffered there. This feeling, broadly, sensuously diffused, as in a masterpiece of Titian, prepares us for the human element to be exhibited.

The foreground of these pictures is occupied by a pair of lovers meeting after the long winter's separation, a dance upon the village green, a young man gazing on the mistress he adores, a disconsolate exile from his home, the courtship of a student and a rustic beauty, or perhaps the grieved and melancholy figure of one whose sweetheart has proved faithless. Such actors in the comedy of life are defined with fervent intensity of touch against the leafy vistas of the scene. The lyrical cry emerges clear and sharp in all that concerns their humanity.

The quality of love expressed is far from being either platonic or chivalrous. It is love of the sensuous, impulsive, appetitive kind, to which we give the name of Pagan. The finest outbursts of passion are emanations from a potent sexual desire. Meanwhile, nothing indicates the character or moral quality of either man or woman. The student and the girl are always *vis-à-vis*, fixed characters in this lyrical love-drama. He calls her Phyllis, Flora, Lydia, Glycerion, Caecilia. He remains unnamed, his physical emotion sufficing for personal description. The divinity presiding over them is Venus. Jove and Danae, Cupid and the Graces, Paris and Helen, follow in her train. All the current classical mythology is laid under cheap contribution. Yet the central emotion, the young man's heart's desire, is so vividly portrayed, that we seem to be overhearing the triumphant ebullition or the melancholy love-lament of a real soul.

X

The sentiment of love is so important in the songs of the Wandering Students, that it may not be superfluous at this point to cull a few emphatic phrases which illustrate the core of their emotion, and to present these in the original Latin.

I may first observe to what a large extent the ideas of spring and of female society were connected at that epoch. Winter was a dreary period, during which a man bore his fate and suffered. He emerged from it into sunshine, brightened by the intercourse with women, which was then made possible. This is how the winter is described : [1] —

> " In omni loco congruo
> Sermonis oblectatio
> Cum sexu femineo
> Evanuit omni modo."

Of the true love-songs, only one refers expressly to the winter season. That, however, is the lyric upon Flora, which contains a detailed study of plastic form in the bold spirit of the Goliardic style.[2]

The particularity with which the personal charms of women are described deserves attention. The portrait of Flora, to which I have just alluded, might be cited as one of the best specimens. But the slightest shades are discriminated, as in this touch : [3] —

[1] *Carm. Bur.*, p. 174.
[2] Ibid., p. 149, translated below in Section xvii.
[3] Ibid., p. 130.

> "Labellulis
> Castigate tumentibus."

One girl has long tawny tresses : *Caesaries subrubea.*
Another is praised for the masses of her dark hair :
Frons nimirum coronata, supercilium nigrata. Roses
and lilies vie, of course, upon the cheeks of all; and
sometimes their sweetness surpasses the lily of the
valley. From time to time a touch of truer poetry
occurs ; as, for instance [1]—

> "O decora super ora
> Belli Absalonis ! "

Or take again the outburst of passion in this stanza,
where both the rhythm and the ponderous Latin
words, together with the abrupt transition from the
third to the fourth line, express a fine exaltation : [2]—

> "Frons et gula, labra, mentum
> Dant amoris alimentum ;
> Crines ejus adamavi,
> Quoniam fuere flavi."

The same kind of enthusiasm is more elaborately
worked out in the following comparisons : [3]—

> "Matutini sideris
> Jubar praeis,
> Et lilium
> Rosaque periere :
> Micat ebur dentium
> Per labium,
> Ut Sirium
> Credat quis enitere."

As might be expected, such lovers were not satisfied
with contemplative pleasures : [4]—

[1] *Carm. Bur.*, p. 200.   [2] Ibid., p. 231.
[3] Ibid., p. 121.   [4] Ibid., p. 135.

> " Visu, colloquio,
> Contactu, basio,
> Frui virgo dederat;
> Sed aberat
> Linea posterior
> Et melior amori,
> Quam nisi transiero,
> De cetero
> Sunt quae dantur alia
> Materia furori."

The conclusion of this song, which, taken in its integrity, deserves to be regarded as typical of what is pagan in this erotic literature, may be studied in the Appendix to *Carmina Burana.*

Occasionally the lover's desire touches a higher point of spirituality :[1]—

> " Non tactu sanabor labiorum,
> Nisi cor unum fiat duorum
> Et idem velle. Vale, flos florum ! "

Occasionally, the sensuous fervour assumes a passionate intensity : [2]—

> " Nocte cum ea si dormiero,
> Si sua labra semel suxero,
> Mortem subire, placenter obire, vitamque finire,
> Libens potero."

Very rarely there is a strong desire expressed for fidelity, as in a beautiful lyric of absence, which I hope to give translated in full in my 17th Section.

But the end to be attained is always such as is summed up in these brief words placed upon a girl's lips : [3]—

[1] *Carm. Bur.*, p.145.   [2] Ibid., p. 230.
[3] Ibid., p. 133.

> " Dulcissime,
>   Totam tibi subdo me."

And the motto of both sexes is this :[1]—

> " Quicquid agant alii,
>   Juvenes amemus."

It may be added, in conclusion, that the sweethearts of our students seem to have been mostly girls of the working and rustic classes, sometimes women of bad fame, rarely married women.   In no case that has come beneath my notice is there any hint that one of them aspired to such amours with noble ladies as distinguished the Troubadours.   A democratic tone, a tone of the proletariate, is rather strangely blent with the display of learning, and with the more than common literary skill apparent in their work.

XI

The drinking-songs are equally spontaneous and fresh.   Anacreon pales before the brilliancy of the Archipoeta when wine is in his veins, and the fountain of the Bacchic chant swells with gushes of strongly emphasised bold double rhymes, each throbbing like a man's firm stroke upon the strings of lyres.   A fine audacity breathes through the praises of the wine-god, sometimes rising to lyric rapture, sometimes sinking to parody and innuendo, but always carrying the bard on rolling wheels along the paths of song.   The reality

[1] *Carm. Bur.*, p. 251.

of the inspiration is indubitable.   These Bacchanalian
choruses have been indited in the tavern, with a crowd
of topers round the poet, with the rattle of the dice-
box ringing in his ears, and with the facile maidens of
his volatile amours draining the wine-cup at his elbow.

Wine is celebrated as the source of pleasure in
social life, provocative of love, parent of poetry : [1]—

> "Bacchus forte superans
> Pectora virorum
> In amorem concitat
> Animos eorum.
>
> Bacchus saepe visitans
> Mulierum genus
> Facit eas subditas
> Tibi, O tu Venus ! "

From his temple, the tavern, water-drinkers and
fastidious persons are peremptorily warned : [2]—

> "Qui potare non potestis,
> Ite procul ab his festis ;
> Non est hic locus modestis :
> Devitantur plus quam pestis."

The tavern is loved better than the church, and a
bowl of wine than the sacramental chalice : [3]—

> " Magis quam ecclesiam
> Diligo tabernam."

> " Mihi sapit dulcius
> Vinum de taberna,
> Quam quod aqua miscuit
> Praesulis pincerna."

---

[1] *Carm. Bur.*, p. 238.   [2] Ibid., p. 240.
[3] Wright's *Walter Mapes*, p. xlv. ; *Carm. Bur.*, p. 69.

As in the love-songs, so in these drinking-songs we
find no lack of mythological allusions. Nor are the
grammatical quibbles, which might also have been
indicated as a defect of the erotic poetry, conspicuous
by absence. But both alike are impotent to break
the spell of evident sincerity. We discount them as
belonging to the euphuism of a certain epoch, and are
rather surprised than otherwise that they should not be
more apparent. The real and serious defect of Goliardic literature is not affectation, but something very
different, which I shall try to indicate in the last
Section of this treatise. Venus and Helen, Liber and
Lyaeus, are but the current coin of poetic diction
common to the whole student class. These Olympian
deities merge without a note of discord into the dim
background of a medieval pothouse or the sylvan
shades of some ephemeral amour, leaving the realism
of natural appetite in either case untouched.

It is by no means the thin and conventional sprink-
ling of classical erudition which makes these poems
of the Goliardi pagan, and reminds the student of
Renaissance art. Conversely, the scholastic plays on
words which they contain do not stamp them but as
medieval. Both of these qualities are *rococo* and
superficial rather than essential and distinctive in their
style. After making due allowances for either element
of oddity, a true connoisseur will gratefully appreciate
the spontaneous note of enjoyment, the disengagement
from ties and duties imposed by temporal respecta-
bility, the frank animalism, which connects these vivid
hymns to Bacchus and Venus with past Aristo-

phanes and future Rabelais.   They celebrate the
eternal presence of mirth-making powers in hearts of
men, apart from time and place and varying dogmas
which do not concern deities of Nature.

XII

The time has now come for me to introduce my
reader to the versions I have made from the songs of
Wandering Students.   I must remind him that, while
the majority of these translations aim at literal exact-
ness and close imitation of the originals in rhyme and
structure, others are more paraphrastic.   It has always
been my creed that a good translation should resemble
a plaster-cast; the English being *plaqué* upon the
original, so as to reproduce its exact form, although it
cannot convey the effects of bronze or marble, which
belong to the material of the work of art.   But this
method has not always seemed to me the most desirable for rendering poems, an eminent quality of which
is facility and spontaneity.   In order to obtain that
quality in our language, the form has occasionally to
be sacrificed.

What Coleridge has reported to have said of
Southey may be applied to a translator.   He too " is
in some sort like an elegant setter of jewels ; the stones
are not his own : he gives them all the advantage of
his art, but not their native brilliancy."   I feel even
more than this when I attempt translation, and reflect
that, unlike the jeweller, it is my doom to reduce the

lustre of the gems I handle, even if I do not substitute paste and pebbles.   Yet I am frequently enticed to repeat experiments, which afterwards I regard in the light of failures.   What allures me first is the pleasure of passing into that intimate familiarity with art which only a copyist or a translator enjoys.   I am next impelled by the desire to fix the attention of readers on things which I admire, and which are possibly beyond their scope of view.   Lastly comes that *ignis fatuus* of the hope, for ever renewed, if also for ever disappointed, that some addition may be made in this way to the wealth of English poetry.   A few exquisite pieces in Latin literature, the Catullian *Ille mi par*, for example, a few in our own, such as Jonson's *Drink to me only with thine eyes*, are translations.   Possibly the miracle of such poetic transmutation may be repeated for me ; possibly an English song may come to birth by my means also.   With this hope in view, the translator is strongly tempted to engraft upon his versions elegances in the spirit of his native language, or to use the motives of the original for improvisations in his own manner.   I must plead guilty to having here and there yielded to this temptation, as may appear upon comparison of my English with the Latin.   All translation is a compromise ; and while being conscious of having to sacrifice much, the translator finds himself often seeking to add something as a makeweight.

I shall divide my specimens into nine Sections. The first will include those which deal with the Order of Wandering Students in general, winding up with the *Confession* ascribed to Golias, the father of the

family. The second, third, fourth, and fifth are
closely connected, since they contain spring-songs,
pastorals, descriptive poems touching upon love, and
erotic lyrics. The sixth Section will be devoted to a
few songs of exile, doubt, and sorrow. In the seventh
we shall reach anacreontics on the theme of wine,
passing in the eighth to parodies and comic pieces.
Four or five serious compositions will close the list in
the ninth Section.

At the end of the book I mean to print a table containing detailed references to the originals of the songs
I have chosen for translation, together with an index
of the principal works that have been published on
this subject.

XIII

The first song which concerns the Order of
Wandering Students in general has been attributed to
the Archipoeta or head-bard of the guild. Whoever
this poet may have been, it is to him that we owe the
Confession of Golias, by far the most spirited composition of the whole Goliardic species. I do not
think the style of the poem on the Order, though it
belongs to a good period, justifies our ascribing it to so
inspired and genial a lyrist.

The argument runs as follows. Just as commission
was given to the Apostles to go forth and preach in
the whole world, so have the Wandering Students a
vocation to travel, and to test the hearts of men wher-

ever they may sojourn. A burlesque turn is given to
this function of the *Vagi*. Yet their consciousness of
a satiric mission, their willingness to pose as critics of
society from the independent vantage-ground of vagabondage, seems seriously hinted at.

The chief part of the song is devoted to a description of the comprehensive nature of the Order, which
receives all sorts and conditions of men, and makes no
distinction of nationality. The habitual poverty of its
members, their favourite pastimes and vices, their love
of gaming and hatred of early rising, are set forth with
some humour.

ON THE ORDER OF WANDERING STUDENTS

No. 1

A T the mandate, Go ye forth,
　　Through the whole world hurry!
Priests tramp out toward south and north,
　　Monks and hermits skurry,
Levites smooth the gospel leave,
　　Bent on ambulation;
Each and all to our sect cleave,
　　Which is life's salvation.

In this sect of ours 'tis writ:
　　Prove all things in season;
Weigh this life and judge of it
　　By your riper reason;

'Gainst all evil clerks be you
  Steadfast in resistance,
Who refuse large tithe and due
  Unto your subsistence.

Marquesses, Bavarians,
  Austrians and Saxons,
Noblemen and chiefs of clans,
  Glorious by your actions!
Listen, comrades all, I pray,
  To these new decretals :
Misers they must meet decay,
  Niggardly gold-beetles.

We the laws of charity
  Found, nor let them crumble ;
For into our order we
  Take both high and humble ;
Rich and poor men we receive,
  In our bosom cherish ;
Welcome those the shavelings leave
  At their doors to perish.

We receive the tonsured monk,
  Let him take his pittance ;
And the parson with his punk,
  If he craves admittance ;
Masters with their bands of boys,
  Priests with high dominion ;
But the scholar who enjoys
  Just one coat's our minion !

This our sect doth entertain
  Just men and unjust ones ;
Halt, lame, weak of limb or brain,
  Strong men and robust ones ;
Those who flourish in their pride,
  Those whom age makes stupid ;
Frigid folk and hot folk fried
  In the fires of Cupid.

Tranquil souls and bellicose,
  Peacemaker and foeman ;
Czech and Hun, and mixed with those
  German, Slav, and Roman ;
Men of middling size and weight,
  Dwarfs and giants mighty ;
Men of modest heart and state,
  Vain men, proud and flighty.

Of the Wanderers' order I
  Tell the Legislature—
They whose life is free and high,
  Gentle too their nature—
They who'd rather scrape a fat
  Dish in gravy swimming,
Than in sooth to marvel at
  Barns with barley brimming.

Now this order, as I ken,
  Is called sect or section,
Since its sectaries are men
  Divers in complexion ;

Therefore *hic* and *haec* and *hoc*
   Suit it in declension,
Since so multiform a flock
   Here finds comprehension.

This our order hath decried
   Matins with a warning ;
For that certain phantoms glide
   In the early morning,
Whereby pass into man's brain
   Visions of vain folly ;
Early risers are insane,
   Racked by melancholy.

This our order doth proscribe
   All the year round matins ;
When they've left their beds, our tribe
   In the tap sing latins ;
There they call for wine for all,
   Roasted fowl and chicken ;
Hazard's threats no hearts appal,
   Though his strokes still thicken.

This our order doth forbid
   Double clothes with loathing :
He whose nakedness is hid
   With one vest hath clothing :
Soon one throws his cloak aside
   At the dice-box' calling ;
Next his girdle is untied,
   While the cards are falling.

What I've said of upper clothes
  To the nether reaches;
They who own a shirt, let those
  Think no more of breeches;
If one boasts big boots to use,
  Let him leave his gaiters;
They who this firm law refuse
  Shall be counted traitors.

No one, none shall wander forth
  Fasting from the table;
If thou'rt poor, from south and north
  Beg as thou art able!
Hath it not been often seen
  That one coin brings many,
When a gamester on the green
  Stakes his lucky penny?

No one on the road should walk
  'Gainst the wind—'tis madness;
Nor in poverty shall stalk
  With a face of sadness;
Let him bear him bravely then,
  Hope sustain his spirit;
After heavy trials men
  Better luck inherit!

While throughout the world you rove,
  Thus uphold your banners;
Give these reasons why you prove
  Hearts of men and manners:

" To reprove the reprobate,
    Probity approving,
  Improbate from approbate
    To remove, I'm moving."

The next song is a lament for the decay of the
Order and the suppression of its privileges. It was
written, to all appearances, at a later date, and is
inferior in style. The Goliardi had already, we
learn from it, exchanged poverty for luxury. Instead
of tramping on the hard hoof, they moved with a
retinue of mounted servants. We seem to trace in the
lament a change from habits of simple vagabondage to
professional dependence, as minstrels and secretaries,
upon men of rank in Church and State, which came
over the Goliardic class. This poem, it may be
mentioned, does not occur in the *Carmina Burana*, nor
is it included among those which bear the name
of Walter Mapes or Map.

ON THE DECAY OF THE ORDER

No. 2

ONCE (it was in days of yore)
    This our order flourished ;
Popes, whom Cardinals adore,
    It with honours nourished ;
Licences desirable
    They gave, nought desiring ;
While our prayers, the beads we tell,
    Served us for our hiring.

Now this order (so time runs)
   Is made tributary ;
With the ruck of Adam's sons
   We must draw and carry ;
Ground by common serfdom down,
   By our debts confounded,
Debts to market-place and town
   With the Jews compounded.

Once ('twas when the simple state
   Of our order lasted)
All men praised us, no man's hate
   Harried us or wasted ;
Rates and taxes on our crew
   There was none to levy ;
But the sect, douce men and true,
   Served God in a bevy.

Now some envious folks, who spy
   Sumptuous equipages,
Horses, litters passing by,
   And a host of pages,
Say, "Unless their purses were
   Quite with wealth o'erflowing,
They could never thus, I swear,
   Round about be going ! "

Such men do not think nor own
   How with toil we bend us,
Not to feed ourselves alone,
   But the folk who tend us :

On all comers, all who come,
    We our substance lavish,
Therefore 'tis a trifling sum
    For ourselves we ravish.

On this subject, at this time,
    What we've said suffices :
Let us leave it, lead the rhyme
    Back to our devices :
We the miseries of this life
    Bear with cheerful spirit,
That Heaven's bounty after strife
    We may duly merit.

'Tis a sign that God the Lord
    Will not let us perish,
Since with scourge and rod and sword
    He our souls doth cherish ;
He amid this vale of woes
    Makes us bear the burden,
That true joys in heaven's repose
    May be ours for guerdon.

Next in order to these poems, which display the
Wandering Students as a class, I will produce two
that exhibit their mode of life in detail. The first is
a begging petition, addressed by a scholar on the tramp
to the great man of the place where he is staying.
The name of the place, as I have already noticed,
is only indicated by an N. The nasal whine of
a suppliant for alms, begging, as Erasmus begged,
not in the name of charity, but of learning, makes

itself heard both in the rhyme and rhythm of the original Latin. I have tried to follow the sing-song doggerel.

A WANDERING STUDENT'S PETITION

No. 3

I, A wandering scholar lad,
    Born for toil and sadness,
Oftentimes am driven by
    Poverty to madness.

Literature and knowledge I
    Fain would still be earning,
Were it not that want of pelf
    Makes me cease from learning.

These torn clothes that cover me
    Are too thin and rotten ;
Oft I have to suffer cold,
    By the warmth forgotten.

Scarce I can attend at church,
    Sing God's praises duly ;
Mass and vespers both I miss,
    Though I love them truly.

Oh, thou pride of N——,
    By thy worth I pray thee
Give the suppliant help in need,
    Heaven will sure repay thee.

Take a mind unto thee now
  Like unto St. Martin ;
Clothe the pilgrim's nakedness,
  Wish him well at parting.

So may God translate your soul
  Into peace eternal,
And the bliss of saints be yours
  In His realm supernal.

The second is a jovial *Song of the Open Road*, throbbing with the exhilaration of young life and madcap impudence.   We must imagine that two vagabond students are drinking together before they part upon their several ways.   One addresses the other as *frater catholice, vir apostolice,* vows to befriend him, and expounds the laws of loyalty which bind the brotherhood together.   To the rest of the world they are a terror and a nuisance.   Honest folk are jeeringly forbidden to beware of the *quadrivium,* which is apt to form a fourfold rogue instead of a scholar in four branches of knowledge.

The Latin metre is so light, careless, and airy, that I must admit an almost complete failure to do it justice in my English version.   The refrain appears intended to imitate a bugle-call.

A SONG OF THE OPEN ROAD

No. 4

WE in our wandering,
  Blithesome and squandering,
    Tara, tantara, teino !

Eat to satiety,
Drink with propriety ;
    Tara, tantara, teino !

Laugh till our sides we split,
Rags on our hides we fit ;
    Tara, tantara, teino !

Jesting eternally,
Quaffing infernally :
    Tara, tantara, teino !

Craft's in the bone of us,
Fear 'tis unknown of us :
    Tara, tantara, teino !

When we're in neediness,
Thieve we with greediness :
    Tara, tantara, teino !

Brother catholical,
Man apostolicla,
    Tara, tantara, teino !

Say what you will have done,
What you ask 'twill be done !
    Tara, tantara, teino !

Folk, fear the toss of the
Horns of philosophy !
                Tara, tantara, teino !

Here comes a quadruple
Spoiler and prodigal !
                Tara, tantara, teino !

License and vanity
Pamper insanity :
                Tara, tantara, teino !

As the Pope bade us do,
Brother to brother's true :
                Tara, tantara, teino !

Brother, best friend, adieu !
Now, I must part from you !
                Tara, tantara, teino !

When will our meeting be ?
Glad shall our greeting be !
                Tara, tantara, teino !

Vows valedictory
Now have the victory ;
                Tara, tantara, teino !

Clasped on each other's breast,
Brother to brother pressed,
                Tara, tantara, teino !

In the fourth place I insert the *Confession of Golias*.
This important composition lays bare the inner nature

of a Wandering Student, describing his vagrant habits,
his volatile and indiscriminate amours, his passion for
the dice-box, his devotion to wine, and the poetic
inspiration he was wont to draw from it.

In England this *Confession* was attributed to Walter
Map; and the famous drinking-song, on which the
Archdeacon of Oxford's reputation principally rests in
modern times, was extracted from the stanzas 11 *et
seq.*[1]   But, though Wright is unwilling to refuse Map
such honour as may accrue to his fame from the composition, we have little reason to regard it as his work.
The song was clearly written at Pavia—a point in-
explicably overlooked by Wright in the note appended
to stanza 9—and the Archbishop-elect of Cologne,
who is appealed to by name in stanza 24, was Reinald
von Dassel, a minister of Frederick Barbarossa.   This
circumstance enables us to determine the date of the
poem between 1162 and 1165.   When the *Confession*
was manipulated for English readers, *Praesul Coven-
trensium, Praesul mihi cognite,* and *O pastor ecclesiae*
were in several MS. redactions substituted for *Electe
Coloniae*.   Instead of *Papiae*, in stanza 8, we read *in
mundo ;* but in stanza 9, where the rhyme required it,
Papiae was left standing—a sufficient indication of
literary rehandling by a clumsy scribe.   In the text of
the *Carmina Burana*, the *Confession* winds up with a
petition that Reinald von Dassel should employ the
poet as a secretary, or should bestow some mark of his
bounty upon him.

---

[1] Wright's *Walter Mapes*, p. xlv.

THE CONFESSION OF GOLIAS

No. 5

BOILING in my spirit's veins
  With fierce indignation,
From my bitterness of soul
  Springs self-revelation :
Framed am I of flimsy stuff,
  Fit for levitation,
Like a thin leaf which the wind
  Scatters from its station.

While it is the wise man's part
  With deliberation
On a rock to base his heart's
  Permanent foundation,
With a running river I
  Find my just equation,
Which beneath the self-same sky
  Hath no habitation.

Carried am I like a ship
  Left without a sailor,
Like a bird that through the air
  Flies where tempests hale her ;
Chains and fetters hold me not,
  Naught avails a jailer ;
Still I find my fellows out
  Toper, gamester, railer.

To my mind all gravity
  Is a grave subjection;
Sweeter far than honey are
  Jokes and free affection.
All that Venus bids me do,
  Do I with erection,
For she ne'er in heart of man
  Dwelt with dull dejection.

Down the broad road do I run,
  As the way of youth is;
Snare myself in sin, and ne'er
  Think where faith and truth is;
Eager far for pleasure more
  Than soul's health, the sooth is,
For this flesh of mine I care,
  Seek not ruth where ruth is.

Prelate, most discreet of priests,
  Grant me absolution!
Dear's the death whereof I die,
  Sweet my dissolution;
For my heart is wounded by
  Beauty's soft suffusion;
All the girls I come not nigh,
  Mine are in illusion.

'Tis most arduous to make
  Nature's self surrender;
Seeing girls, to blush and be
  Purity's defender!

We young men our longings ne'er
  Shall to stern law render,
Or preserve our fancies from
  Bodies smooth and tender.

Who, when into fire he falls,
  Keeps himself from burning?
Who within Pavia's walls
  Fame of chaste is earning?
Venus with her finger calls
  Youths at every turning,
Snares them with her eyes, and thralls
  With her amorous yearning.

If you brought Hippolitus
  To Pavia Sunday,
He'd not be Hippolitus
  On the following Monday;
Venus there keeps holiday
  Every day as one day;
'Mid these towers in no tower dwells
  Venus Verecunda.

In the second place I own
  To the vice of gaming:
Cold indeed outside I seem,
  Yet my soul is flaming:
But when once the dice-box hath
  Stripped me to my shaming,
Make I songs and verses fit
  For the world's acclaiming.

In the third place, I will speak
  Of the tavern's pleasure ;
For I never found nor find
  There the least displeasure ;
Nor shall find it till I greet
  Angels without measure,
Singing requiems for the souls
  In eternal leisure.

In the public-house to die
  Is my resolution ;
Let wine to my lips be nigh
  At life's dissolution :
That will make the angels cry,
  With glad elocution,
" Grant this toper, God on high,
  Grace and absolution ! "

With the cup the soul lights up,
  Inspirations flicker ;
Nectar lifts the soul on high
  With its heavenly ichor :
To my lips a sounder taste
  Hath the tavern's liquor
Than the wine a village clerk
  Waters for the vicar.

Nature gives to every man
  Some gift serviceable ;
Write I never could nor can
  Hungry at the table ;

Fasting, any stripling to
  Vanquish me is able ;
Hunger, thirst, I liken to
  Death that ends the fable.

Nature gives to every man
  Gifts as she is willing ;
I compose my verses when
  Good wine I am swilling,
Wine the best for jolly guest
  Jolly hosts are filling ;
From such wine rare fancies fine
  Flow like dews distilling.

Such my verse is wont to be
  As the wine I swallow ;
No ripe thoughts enliven me
  While my stomach's hollow ;
Hungry wits on hungry lips
  Like a shadow follow,
But when once I'm in my cups,
  I can beat Apollo.

Never to my spirit yet
  Flew poetic vision
Until first my belly had
  Plentiful provision ;
Let but Bacchus in the brain
  Take a strong position,
Then comes Phoebus flowing in
  With a fine precision.

There are poets, worthy men,
　　Shrink from public places,
And in lurking-hole or den
　　Hide their pallid faces;
There they study, sweat, and woo
　　Pallas and the Graces,
But bring nothing forth to view
　　Worth the girls' embraces.

Fasting, thirsting, toil the bards,
　　Swift years flying o'er them;
Shun the strife of open life,
　　Tumults of the forum;
They, to sing some deathless thing,
　　Lest the world ignore them,
Die the death, expend their breath,
　　Drowned in dull decorum.

Lo! my frailties I've betrayed,
　　Shown you every token,
Told you what your servitors
　　Have against me spoken;
But of those men each and all
　　Leave their sins unspoken,
Though they play, enjoy to-day,
　　Scorn their pledges broken.

Now within the audience-room
　　Of this blessèd prelate,
Sent to hunt out vice, and from
　　Hearts of men expel it;

Let him rise, nor spare the bard,
   Cast at him a pellet:
He whose heart knows not crime's smart,
   Show my sin and tell it!

I have uttered openly
   All I knew that shamed me,
And have spued the poison forth
   That so long defamed me;
Of my old ways I repent,
   New life hath reclaimed me;
God beholds the heart—'twas man
   Viewed the face and blamed me.

Goodness now hath won my love,
   I am wroth with vices;
Made a new man in my mind,
   Lo, my soul arises!
Like a babe new milk I drink—
   Milk for me suffices,
Lest my heart should longer be
   Filled with vain devices.

Thou Elect of fair Cologne,
   Listen to my pleading!
Spurn not thou the penitent;
   See, his heart is bleeding!
Give me penance! what is due
   For my faults exceeding
I will bear with willing cheer,
   All thy precepts heeding.

Lo, the lion, king of beasts,
　Spares the meek and lowly ;
Toward submissive creatures he
　Tames his anger wholly.
Do the like, ye powers of earth,
　Temporal and holy !
Bitterness is more than's right
　When 'tis bitter solely.

XIV

Having been introduced to the worshipful order of vagrants both in their collective and in their personal capacity, we will now follow them to the woods and fields in spring.   It was here that they sought love-adventures and took pastime after the restraints of winter.

The spring-songs are all, in the truest sense of the word, *lieder*—lyrics for music.   Their affinities of form and rhythm are less with ecclesiastical verse than with the poetry of the Minnesinger and the Troubadour. Sometimes we are reminded of the French *pastourelle*, sometimes of the rustic ditty, with its monotonous refrain.

The exhilaration of the season which they breathe has something of the freshness of a lark's song, some-thing at times of the richness of the nightingale's lament.   The defect of the species may be indicated in a single phrase.   It is a tedious reiteration of commonplaces in the opening stanzas.   Here, however, is a lark-song.

SPRING

WELCOME TO SPRING

No. 6

SPRING is coming! longed-for spring
   Now his joy discloses;
On his fair brow in a ring
   Bloom empurpled roses!
Birds are gay; how sweet their lay!
   Tuneful is the measure;
The wild wood grows green again,
Songsters change our winter's pain
   To a mirthful pleasure.

Now let young men gather flowers,
   On their foreheads bind them,
Maidens pluck them from the bowers,
   Then, when they have twined them,
Breathe perfume from bud and bloom,
   Where young love reposes,
And into the meadows so
All together laughing go,
   Crowned with ruddy roses.

Here again the nightingale's song, contending with
the young man's heart's lament of love, makes itself
heard.

THE LOVER AND THE NIGHTINGALE

No. 7

THESE hours of spring are jolly;
         Maidens, be gay!
Shake off dull melancholy,
         Ye lads, to-day!
   Oh! all abloom am I!
   It is a maiden love that makes me sigh,
   A new, new love it is wherewith I die!

The nightingale is singing
         So sweet a lay!
Her glad voice heavenward flinging—
         No check, no stay.

Flower of girls love-laden
         Is my sweetheart;
Of roses red the maiden
         For whom I smart.

The promise that she gives me
         Makes my heart bloom;
If she denies, she drives me
         Forth to the gloom.

My maid, to me relenting,
         Is fain for play;
Her pure heart, unconsenting,
         Saith, " Lover, stay! "

Hush, Philomel, thy singing,
     This little rest!
Let the soul's song rise ringing
     Up from the breast!

In desolate Decembers
     Man bides his time:
Spring stirs the slumbering embers;
     Love-juices climb.

Come, mistress, come, my maiden!
     Bring joy to me!
Come, come, thou beauty-laden!
     I die for thee!
     O all abloom am I!
     It is a maiden love that makes me sigh,
     A new, new love it is wherewith I die!

There is a very pretty *Invitation to Youth*, the refrain of which, though partly undecipherable, seems to indicate an Italian origin. I have thought it well to omit this refrain; but it might be rendered thus, maintaining the strange and probably corrupt reading of the last line :—

    " List, my fair, list, *bela mia*,
      To the thousand charms of Venus!
      Da hizevaleria."

THE INVITATION TO YOUTH

No. 8

TAKE your pleasure, dance and play,
Each with other while ye may :
Youth is nimble, full of grace ;
Age is lame, of tardy pace.

We the wars of love should wage,
Who are yet of tender age ;
'Neath the tents of Venus dwell
All the joys that youth loves well.

Young men kindle heart's desire ;
You may liken them to fire :
Old men frighten love away
With cold frost and dry decay.

A roundelay, which might be styled the *Praise of
May* or the exhortation to be liberal in love by *The
Example of the Rose*, shall follow.

THE EXAMPLE OF THE ROSE

No. 9

WINTER'S untruth yields at last,
Spring renews old mother earth ;
Angry storms are overpast,
Sunbeams fill the air with mirth ;
Pregnant, ripening unto birth,
All the world reposes.

Our delightful month of May,
   Not by birth, but by degree,
Took the first place, poets say;
   Since the whole year's cycle he,
   Youngest, loveliest, leads with glee,
      And the cycle closes.

From the honours of the rose
   They decline, the rose abuse,
Who, when roses red unclose,
   Seek not their own sweets to use;
   'Tis with largess, liberal dues,
      That the rose discloses.

Taught to wanton, taught to play,
   By the young year's wanton flower,
We will take no heed to-day,
   Have no thought for thrift this hour;
   Thrift, whose uncongenial power
      Laws on youth imposes.

Another song, blending the praises of spring with a
little pagan vow to Cupid, has in the original Latin a
distinction and purity of outline which might be almost
called Horatian.

THE VOW TO CUPID
No. 10

WINTER, now thy spite is spent,
   Frost and ice and branches bent!
Fogs and furious storms are o'er,
Sloth and torpor, sorrow frore,
Pallid wrath, lean discontent.

Comes the graceful band of May!
Cloudless shines the limpid day,
Shine by night the Pleiades;
While a grateful summer breeze
Makes the season soft and gay.

Golden Love! shine forth to view!
Souls of stubborn men subdue!
See me bend! what is thy mind?
Make the girl thou givest kind,
And a leaping ram's thy due!

O the jocund face of earth,
Breathing with young grassy birth!
Every tree with foliage clad,
Singing birds in greenwood glad,
Flowering fields for lovers' mirth!

Nor is the next far below it in the same qualities of
neatness and artistic brevity.

A-MAYING

No. 11

NOW the fields are laughing; now the maids
Take their pastime; laugh the leafy glades:
Now the summer days are blooming,
And the flowers their chaliced lamps for
love illuming.

Fruit-trees blossom ; woods grow green again ;
Winter's rage is past : O ye young men,
    With the May-bloom shake off sadness !
    Love is luring you to join the maidens' gladness.

Let us then together sport and play ;
Cytherea bids the young be gay :
    Laughter soft and happy voices,
    Hope and love invite to mirth when May
        rejoices.

All the spring is in the lyric next upon my list.

THE RETURN OF SPRING

No. 12

SPRING returns, the glad new-comer,
    Bringing pleasure, banning pain :
Meadows bloom with early summer,
    And the sun shines out again :
All sad thoughts and passions vanish ;
Plenteous Summer comes to banish
    Winter with his starveling train.

Hails and snows and frosts together
    Melt and thaw like dews away ;
While the spring in cloudless weather
    Sucks the breast of jocund May ;
Sad's the man and born for sorrow
Who can live not, dares not borrow
    Gladness from a summer's day.

Full of joy and jubilation,
   Drunk with honey of delight,
Are the lads whose aspiration
   Is the palm of Cupid's fight!
Youths, we'll keep the laws of Venus,
And with joy and mirth between us
   Live and love like Paris wight!

The next has the same accent of gladness, though
it is tuned to a somewhat softer and more meditative
note of feeling.

THE SWEETNESS OF THE SPRING

No. 13

VERNAL hours are sweet as clover,
   With love's honey running over;
Every heart on this earth burning
Finds new birth with spring's returning.

In the spring-time blossoms flourish,
Fields drink moisture, heaven's dews nourish;
Now the griefs of maidens, after
Dark days, turn to love and laughter.

Whoso love, are loved, together
Seek their pastime in spring weather;
And, with time and place agreeing,
Clasp, kiss, frolic, far from seeing.

Gradually the form of the one girl whom the lyrist
loves emerges from this wealth of description.

THE SUIT TO PHYLLIS

No. 14

HAIL ! thou longed-for month of May,
　　Dear to lovers every day !
Thou that kindlest hour by hour
Life in man and bloom in bower !
O ye crowds of flowers and hues
That with joy the sense confuse,
Hail ! and to our bosom bring
Bliss and every jocund thing !
Sweet the concert of the birds ;
Lovers listen to their words :
For sad winter hath gone by,
And a soft wind blows on high.

Earth hath donned her purple vest,
Fields with laughing flowers are dressed,
Shade upon the wild wood spreads,
Trees lift up their leafy heads ;
Nature in her joy to-day
Bids all living things be gay ;
Glad her face and fair her grace
Underneath the sun's embrace !
Venus stirs the lover's brain,
With life's nectar fills his vein,
Pouring through his limbs the heat
Which makes pulse and passion beat.

O how happy was the birth
When the loveliest soul on earth
Took the form and life of thee,
Shaped in all felicity !
O how yellow is thy hair !
There is nothing wrong, I swear,
In the whole of thee ; thou art
Framed to fill a loving heart !
Lo, thy forehead queenly crowned,
And the eyebrows dark and round,
Curved like Iris at the tips,
Down the dark heavens when she slips !

Red as rose and white as snow
Are thy cheeks that pale and glow ;
'Mid a thousand maidens thou
Hast no paragon, I vow.
Round thy lips and red as be
Apples on the apple-tree ;
Bright thy teeth as any star ;
Soft and low thy speeches are ;
Long thy hand, and long thy side,
And the throat thy breasts divide ;
All thy form beyond compare
Was of God's own art the care.

Sparks of passion sent from thee
Set on fire the heart of me ;
Thee beyond all whom I know
I must love for ever so.
Lo, my heart to dust will burn
Unless thou this flame return ;

Still the fire will last, and I,
Living now, at length shall die !
Therefore, Phyllis, hear me pray,
Let us twain together play,
Joining lip to lip and breast
Unto breast in perfect rest !

The lover is occasionally bashful, sighing at a distance.

MODEST LOVE

No. 15

SUMMER sweet is coming in ;
Now the pleasant days begin ;
Phoebus rules the earth at last ;
For sad winter's reign is past.

Wounded with the love alone
Of one girl, I make my moan :
Grief pursues me till she bend
Unto me and condescend.

Take thou pity on my plight !
With my heart thy heart unite !
In my love thy own love blending,
Finding thus of life the ending!

Occasionally his passion assumes a romantic tone, as is the case with the following *Serenade* to a girl called Flos-de-spina in the Latin. Whether that was her

real name, or was only used for poetical purposes, does
not admit of debate now.   Anyhow, Flos-de-spina,
Fior-di-spina, Fleur-d'épine, and English Flower-o'-
the-thorn are all of them pretty names for a girl.

THE SERENADE TO FLOWER-
O'-THE-THORN

No. 16

THE blithe young year is upward steering,
   Wild winter dwindles, disappearing ;
The short, short days are growing longer,
Rough weather yields and warmth is stronger.
   Since January dawned, my mind
   Waves hither, thither, love-inclined
   For one whose will can loose or bind.

Prudent and very fair the maiden,
Than rose or lily more love-laden ;
Stately of stature, lithe and slender,
There's naught so exquisite and tender.
   The Queen of France is not so dear ;
   Death to my life comes very near
   If Flower-o'-the-thorn be not my cheer.

The Queen of Love my heart is killing
With her gold arrow pain-distilling ;
The God of Love with torches burning
Lights pyre on pyre of ardent yearning.
   She is the girl for whom I'd die ;
   I want none dearer, far or nigh,
   Though grief on grief upon me lie.

I with her love am thralled and taken,
Whose flower doth flower, bud, bloom, and waken ;
Sweet were the labour, light the burden,
Could mouth kiss mouth for wage and guerdon.
      No touch of lips my wound can still,
      Unless two hearts grow one, one will,
      One longing !   Flower of flowers, farewell !

Once at least we find him writing in absence to hi
mistress, and imploring her fidelity. This ranks among
the most delicate in sentiment of the whole series.

THE LOVE-LETTER IN SPRING

No. 17

NOW the sun is streaming,
      Clear and pure his ray ;
April's glad face beaming
      On our earth to-day.
Unto love returneth
      Every gentle mind ;
And the boy-god burneth
      Jocund hearts to bind.

All this budding beauty,
      Festival array,
Lays on us the duty
      To be blithe and gay.
Trodden ways are known, love !
      And in this thy youth,
To retain thy own love
      Were but faith and truth.

In faith love me solely,
　　Mark the faith of me,
From thy whole heart wholly,
　　From the soul of thee.
At this time of bliss, dear,
　　I am far away ;
Those who love like this, dear,
　　Suffer every day !

At one time he seems upon the point of clasping his
felicity.

A SPRING DITTY

No. 18

IN the spring, ah happy day !
Underneath a leafy spray
With her sister stands my may.
　　　　O sweet love !
　　　　He who now is reft of thee
　　　　Poor is he !

Ah, the trees, how fair they flower
Birds are singing in the bower ;
Maidens feel of love the power.
　　　　O sweet love !

See the lilies, how they blow !
And the maidens row by row
Praise the best of gods below.
　　　　O sweet love !

If I held my sweetheart now,
In the wood beneath the bough,
I would kiss her, lip and brow.
  O sweet love !
  He who now is reft of thee,
  Poor is he !

At another time he has clasped it, but he trembles
lest it should escape him.

LOVE-DOUBTS

No. 19

WITH so sweet a promise given
  All my bosom burneth ;
Hope uplifts my heart to heaven,
 Yet the doubt returneth,
Lest perchance that hope should be
Crushed and shattered suddenly.

On one girl my fancy so,
 On one star, reposes ;
Her sweet lips with honey flow
 And the scent of roses :
In her smile I laugh, and fire
Fills me with her love's desire.

Love in measure over-much
 Strikes man's soul with anguish ;
Anxious love's too eager touch
 Makes man fret and languish :

Thus in doubt and grief I pine ;
Pain more sure was none than mine.

Burning in love's fiery flood,
   Lo, my life is wasted !
Such the fever of my blood
   That I scarce have tasted
Mortal bread and wine, but sup
Like a god love's nectar-cup.

The village dance forms an important element in
he pleasures of the season.   Here is a pretty picture
in two stanzas of a linden sheltering some Suabian
meadow.

THE VILLAGE DANCE

No. 20

WIDE the lime-tree to the air
      Spreads her boughs and foliage fair ;
   Thyme beneath is growing
On the verdant meadow where
   Dancers' feet are going.

Through the grass a little spring
Runs with jocund murmuring ;
   All the place rejoices ;
Cooling zephyrs breathe and sing
   With their summer voices.

I have freely translated a second, which presents a
more elaborate picture of a similar scene.

THE VILLAGE DANCE

LOVE AMONG THE MAIDENS

No. 21

YONDER choir of virgins see
    Through the spring advancing,
Where the sun's warmth, fair and free,
    From the green leaves glancing,
Weaves a lattice of light gloom
    And soft sunbeams o'er us,
'Neath the linden-trees in bloom,
    For the Cyprian chorus.

In this vale where blossoms blow,
    Blooming, summer-scented,
'Mid the lilies row by row,
    Spreads a field flower-painted.
Here the blackbirds through the dale
    Each to each are singing,
And the jocund nightingale
    Her fresh voice is flinging.

See the maidens crowned with rose
    Sauntering through the grasses!
Who could tell the mirth of those
    Laughing, singing lasses?
Or with what a winning grace
    They their charms discover,
Charms of form and blushing face,
    To the gazing lover?

Down the flowery greenwood glade
As I chanced to wander,
From bright eyes a serving-maid
Shot Love's arrows yonder ;
I for her, 'mid all the crew
Of the girls of Venus,
Wait and yearn until I view
Love spring up between us.

Another lyric of complicated rhyming structure
introduces a not dissimilar motive, with touches that
seem, in like manner, to indicate its German origin.
It may be remarked that the lover's emotion has here
unusual depth, a strain of *sehnsucht;* and the picture
of the mother followed by her daughter in the country-
dance suggests the domesticity of Northern races.

AT THE VILLAGE DANCE

No. 22

MEADOWS bloom, in Winter's room
Reign the Loves and Graces,
With their gift of buds that lift
Bright and laughing faces;
'Neath the ray of genial May,
Shining, glowing, blushing, growing,
They the joys of spring are showing
In their manifold array.

Song-birds sweet the season greet,
  Tune their merry voices ;
Sound the ways with hymns of praise,
  Every lane rejoices.
On the bough in greenwood now
  Flowers are springing, perfumes flinging,
  While young men and maids are clinging
To the loves they scarce avow.

O'er the grass together pass
  Bands of lads love-laden :
Row by row in bevies go
  Bride and blushing maiden.
See with glee 'neath linden-tree,
  Where the dancing girls are glancing,
  How the matron is advancing !
At her side her daughter see !

She's my own, for whom alone,
  If fate wills, I'll tarry ;
Young May-moon, or late or soon,
  'Tis with her I'd marry !
Now with sighs I watch her rise,
  She the purely loved, the surely
  Chosen, who my heart securely
Turns from grief to Paradise.

In her sight with heaven's own light
  Like the gods I blossom ;
Care for nought till she be brought
  Yielding to my bosom.

Thirst divine my soul doth pine
  To behold her and enfold her,
    With clasped arms alone to hold her
In Love's holy hidden shrine.

But the theme of the dance is worked up with even greater elaboration and a more studied ingenuity of rhyme and rhythm in the following characteristic song. This has the true accent of what may be called the *Musa Vagabundula*, and is one of the best lyrics of the series :—

INVITATION TO THE DANCE

No. 23

CAST aside dull books and thought;
    Sweet is folly, sweet is play :
Take the pleasure Spring hath brought
    In youth's opening holiday !
Right it is old age should ponder
    On grave matters fraught with care ;
Tender youth is free to wander,
    Free to frolic light as air.
        Like a dream our prime is flown,
            Prisoned in a study :
        Sport and folly are youth's own,
            Tender youth and ruddy.

Lo, the Spring of life slips by,
    Frozen Winter comes apace ;
Strength is 'minished silently,
    Care writes wrinkles on our face :

Blood dries up and courage fails us,
   Pleasures dwindle, joys decrease,
Till old age at length assails us
   With his troop of illnesses.
        Like a dream our prime is flown,
          Prisoned in a study ;
        Sport and folly are youth's own,
          Tender youth and ruddy.

Live we like the gods above ;
   This is wisdom, this is truth :
Chase the joys of tender love
   In the leisure of our youth !
Keep the vows we swore together,
   Lads, obey that ordinance ;
Seek the fields in sunny weather,
   Where the laughing maidens dance.
        Like a dream our prime is flown,
          Prisoned in a study ;
        Sport and folly are youth's own,
          Tender youth and ruddy.

There the lad who lists may see
   Which among the maids is kind :
There young limbs deliciously
   Flashing through the dances wind :
While the girls their arms are raising,
   Moving, winding o'er the lea,
Still I stand and gaze, and gazing
   They have stolen the soul of me !

Like a dream our prime is flown,
    Prisoned in a study ;
Sport and folly are youth's own,
    Tender youth and ruddy.

XV

A separate Section can be devoted to songs in the
manner of the early French pastoral.   These were
fashionable at a remote period in all parts of Europe ;
and I have already had occasion, in another piece of
literary history, to call attention to the Italian madrigals
of the fourteenth century composed in this species.[1]
Their point is mainly this : A man of birth and edu-
cation, generally a dweller in the town, goes abroad
into the fields, lured by fair spring weather, and makes
love among trees to a country wench.

The *Vagi* turn the pastoral to their own purpose,
and always represent the greenwood lover as a *clericus*.
One of these rural pieces has a pretty opening stanza :—

" When the sweet Spring was ascending,
    Not yet May, at April's ending,
    While the sun was heavenward wending,
    Stood a girl of grace transcending
    Underneath the green bough, sending
        Songs aloft with pipings."

Another gives a slightly comic turn to the chief
incident.

[1] See *Renaissance in Italy*, vol. iv. p. 156.

A PASTORAL

No. 24

THERE went out in the dawning light
    A little rustic maiden;
Her flock so white, her crook so slight,
    With fleecy new wool laden.

Small is the flock, and there you'll see
    The she-ass and the wether;
This goat's a he, and that's a she,
    The bull-calf and the heifer.

She looked upon the green sward, where
    A student lay at leisure:
"What do you there, young sir, so fair?"
    "Come, play with me, my treasure!"

A third seems to have been written in the South,
perhaps upon the shores of one of the Italian lakes—
Como or Garda.

THE MULBERRY-GATHERER

No. 25

IN the summer's burning heat,
    When the flowers were blooming sweet,
I had chosen, as 'twas meet,
'Neath an olive bough my seat;
Languid with the glowing day,
Lazy, careless, apt for play.

Stood the tree in fields where grew
Painted flowers of every hue,
Grass that flourished with the dew,
Fresh with shade where breezes blew ;
Plato, with his style so rare,
Could not paint a spot more fair.

Runs a babbling brook hard by,
Chants the nightingale on high ;
Water-nymphs with song reply.
" Sure, 'tis Paradise," I cry ;
For I know not any place
Of a sweeter, fresher grace.

While I take my solace here,
And in solace find good cheer,
Shade from summer, coolness dear,
Comes a shepherd maiden near—
Fairer, sure, there breathes not now—
Plucking mulberries from the bough.

Seeing her, I loved her there :
Venus did the trick, I'll swear !
" Come, I am no thief, to scare,
Rob, or murder unaware ;
I and all I have are thine,
Thou than Flora more divine ! "

But the girl made answer then :
" Never played I yet with men ;
Cruel to me are my kin :
My old mother scolds me when
In some little thing I stray :—
Hold, I prithee, sir, to-day ! "

A fourth, consisting of a short conventional introduction in praise of Spring, followed by a dialogue
between a young man and a girl, in which the metre
changes for the last two stanzas, may be classed among
the pastorals, although it is a somewhat irregular
example of the species.

THE WOOING

No. 26

ALL the woods are now in flower,
Song-birds sing in field and bower,
Orchards their white blossoms shower :
Lads, make merry in Love's hour !

Sordid grief hath flown away,
Fervid Love is here to-day ;
He will tame without delay
Those who love not while they may.

He. " Fairest maiden, list to me ;
Do not thus disdainful be ;
Scorn and anger disagree
With thy youth, and injure thee.

I am weaker than thou art ;
Mighty Love hath pierced my heart ;
Scarce can I endure his dart :
Lest I die, heal, heal my smart ! "

She. " Why d' you coax me, suitor blind ?
What you seek you will not find ;

I'm too young for love to bind ;
Such vain trifles vex my mind.

Is't your will with me to toy ?
I'll not mate with man or boy :
Like the Phœnix, to enjoy
Single life shall be my joy."

He. "Yet Love is tyrannous,
Harsh, fierce, imperious !
He who man's heart can thus
   Shatter, may make to bow
   Maidens as stern as thou ! "

She. "Now by your words I'm 'ware
What you wish, what you are ;
You know love well, I swear !
   So I'll be loved by you ;
   Now I'm on fire too ! "

XVI

Some semi-descriptive pieces, which connect the
songs of Spring with lyrics of a more purely personal
emotion, can boast of rare beauty in the original.

The most striking of these, upon the theme of
Sleep and Love, I have tried to render in trochaic
verse, feeling it impossible, without knowledge of the
medieval melody, to reproduce its complicated and
now only half-intelligible rhythms.

SLEEP AND LOVE

A DESCANT UPON SLEEP AND LOVE

No. 27

WHEN the lamp of Cynthia late
    Rises in her silver state,
Through her brother's roseate light,
Blushing on the brows of night;
Then the pure ethereal air
Breathes with zephyr blowing fair;
Clouds and vapours disappear.
As with chords of lute or lyre,
Soothed the spirits now respire,
And the heart revives again
Which once more for love is fain.
But the orient evening star
Sheds with influence kindlier far
Dews of sweet sleep on the eye
Of o'er-tired mortality.

Oh, how blessed to take and keep
Is the antidote of sleep!
Sleep that lulls the storms of care
And of sorrow unaware,
Creeping through the closèd doors
Of the eyes, and through the pores
Breathing bliss so pure and rare
That with love it may compare.

Then the god of dreams doth bring
To the mind some restful thing,

Breezes soft that rippling blow
O'er ripe cornfields row by row,
Murmuring rivers round whose brim
Silvery sands the swallows skim,
Or the drowsy circling sound
Of old mill-wheels going round,
Which with music steal the mind
And the eyes in slumber bind.

When the deeds of love are done
Which bland Venus had begun,
Languor steals with pleasant strain
Through the chambers of the brain,
Eyes 'neath eyelids gently tired
Swim and seek the rest desired.
How deliciously at last
Into slumber love hath passed !
But how sweeter yet the way
Which leads love again to play !

From the soothed limbs upward spread
Glides a mist divinely shed,
Which invades the heart and head :
Drowsily it veils the eyes,
Bending toward sleep's paradise,
And with curling vapour round
Fills the lids, the senses swound,
Till the visual ray is bound
By those ministers which make
Life renewed in man awake.

Underneath the leafy shade
Of a tree in quiet laid,

While the nightingale complains
Singing of her ancient pains,
Sweet it is still hours to pass,
But far sweeter on the grass
With a buxom maid to play
All a summer's holiday.
When the scent of herb and flower
Breathes upon the silent hour,
When the rose with leaf and bloom
Spreads a couch of pure perfume,
Then the grateful boon of sleep
Falls with satisfaction deep,
Showering dews our eyes above,
Tired with honeyed strife of love.

In how many moods the mind
Of poor lovers, weak and blind,
Wavers like the wavering wind !
As a ship in darkness lost,
Without anchor tempest-tossed,
So with hope and fear imbued
It roams in great incertitude
Love's tempestuous ocean-flood.

A portion of this descant finds an echo in another
lyric of the *Carmina Burana* :—

" With young leaves the wood is new ;
    Now the nightingale is singing ;
And field-flowers of every hue
    On the sward their bloom are flinging.
Sweet it is to brush the dew
    From wild lawns and woody places !

> Sweeter yet to wreathe the rose
>   With the lily's virgin graces;
> But the sweetest sweet man knows,
>   Is to woo a girl's embraces."

The most highly wrought of descriptive poems in this species is the *Dispute of Flora and Phyllis*, which occurs both in the *Carmina Burana* and in the English MSS. edited by Wright. The motive of the composition is as follows:—Two girls wake in the early morning, and go out to walk together through the fields. Each of them is in love; but Phyllis loves a soldier, Flora loves a scholar. They interchange confidences, the one contending with the other for the superiority of her own sweetheart.

Having said so much, I will present the first part of the poem in the English version I have made.

FLORA AND PHYLLIS

Part I

No. 28

IN the spring-time, when the skies
    Cast off winter's mourning,
And bright flowers of every hue
    Earth's lap are adorning,
At the hour when Lucifer
    Gives the stars their warning,
Phyllis woke, and Flora too,
    In the early morning.

Both the girls were fain to go
   Forth in sunny weather,
For love-laden bosoms throw
   Sleep off like a feather;
Then with measured steps and slow
   To the fields together
Went they, seeking pastime new
   'Mid the flowers and heather.

Both were virgins, both, I ween,
   Were by birth princesses;
Phyllis let her locks flow free,
   Flora trained her tresses.
Not like girls they went, but like
   Heavenly holinesses;
And their faces shone like dawn
   'Neath the day's caresses.

Equal beauty, equal birth,
   These fair maidens mated;
Youthful were the years of both,
   And their minds elated;
Yet they were a pair unpaired,
   Mates by strife unmated;
For one loved a clerk, and one
   For a knight was fated.

Naught there was of difference
   'Twixt them to the seeing,
All alike, within without,
   Seemed in them agreeing;

With one garb, one cast of mind,
  And one mode of being,
Only that they could not love
  Save with disagreeing.

In the tree-tops overhead
  A spring breeze was blowing,
And the meadow lawns around
  With green grass were growing ;
Through the grass a rivulet
  From the hill was flowing,
Lively, with a pleasant sound
  Garrulously going.

That the girls might suffer less
  From the noon resplendent,
Near the stream a spreading pine
  Rose with stem ascendant ;
Crowned with boughs and leaves aloft,
  O'er the fields impendent ;
From all heat on every hand
  Airily defendent.

On the sward the maidens sat,
  Naught that seat surpasses ;
Phyllis near the rivulet,
  Flora 'mid the grasses ;
Each into the chamber sweet
  Of her own soul passes,
Love divides their thoughts, and wounds
  With his shafts the lasses.

Love within the breast of each,
    Hidden, unsuspected,
Lurks and draws forth sighs of grief
    From their hearts dejected :
Soon their ruddy cheeks grow pale,
    Conscious, love-affected ;
Yet their passion tells no tale,
    By soft shame protected.

Phyllis now doth overhear
    Flora softly sighing :
Flora with like luck detects
    Sigh to sigh replying.
Thus the girls exchange the game,
    Each with other vying ;
Till the truth leaps out at length,
    Plain beyond denying.

Long this interchange did last
    Of mute conversation ;
All of love-sighs fond and fast
    Was that dissertation.
Love was in their minds, and Love
    Made their lips his station ;
Phyllis then, while Flora smiled,
    Opened her oration.

" Soldier brave, my love ! " she said,
    " Where is now my Paris ?
Fights he in the field, or where
    In the wide world tarries ?

> Oh, the soldier's life, I swear,
>   All life's glory carries;
> Only valour clothed in arms
>   With Dame Venus marries!"

Phyllis thus opens the question whether a soldier or a scholar be the fitter for love. Flora responds, and for some time they conduct the dispute in true scholastic fashion. Being unable to settle it between themselves, they resolve to seek out Love himself, and to refer the matter to his judgment. One girl mounts a mule, the other a horse; and these are no ordinary animals, for Neptune reared one beast as a present to Venus, Vulcan forged the metal-work of bit and saddle, Minerva embroidered the trappings, and so forth. After a short journey they reach the Garden of Love, which is described with a truly luxuriant wealth of imagery. It resembles some of the earlier Renaissance pictures, especially one of great excellence by a German artist which I once saw in a dealer's shop at Venice, and which ought now to grace a public gallery.

FLORA AND PHYLLIS

PART III

No. 29

ON their steeds the ladies ride,
    Two fair girls and slender;
Modest are their eyes and mild,
    And their cheeks are tender.

Thus young lilies break the sheath,
  Budding roses render
Blushes, and twinned pairs of stars
  Climb the heavens with splendour.

Toward Love's Paradise they fare,
  Such, I ween, their will is;
While the strife between the pair
  Turns their cheeks to lilies;
Phyllis Flora flouts, and fair
  Flora flouteth Phyllis;
Flora's hand a hawk doth bear,
  And a goshawk Phyllis.

After a short space they came
  Where a grove was growing;
At the entrance of the same
  Rills with murmur flowing;
There the wind with myrrh and spice
  Redolent was blowing,
Sounds of timbrel, harp, and lyre
  Through the branches going.

All the music man could make
  There they heard in plenty;
Timbrel, psaltery, lyre, and lute,
  Harp and viol dainty;
Voices that in part-song meet
  Choiring forte, lente;
Sounds the diatesseron,
  Sounds the diapente.

All the tongues of all the birds
    With full cry were singing;
There the blackbird's melody
    Sweet and true was ringing;
Wood-dove, lark, and thrush on high
    Jocund anthems flinging,
With the nightingale, who still
    To her grief was clinging.

When the girls drew nigh the grove,
    Some fear came upon them;
Further as they fared, the charm
    Of the pleasance won them;
All the birds so sweetly sang
    That a spell was on them,
And their bosoms warmed with love
    At the welcome shown them.

Man would be immortal if
    He could there be dwelling:
Every branch on every tree
    With ripe fruit is swelling;
All the ways with nard and myrrh
    And with spice are smelling:
How divine the Master is
    All the house is telling.

Blithesome bands arrest their gaze,
    Youths and maidens dancing;
Bodies beauteous as the stars,
    Eyes with heaven's light glancing;

And the bosoms of the girls,
    At the sight entrancing,
Leap to view such marvels new,
    Joy with joy enhancing!

They their horses check, and light,
    Moved with sudden pleasure;
Half forget what brought them here,
    Thralled by love and leisure;
Till once more the nightingale
    Tuned her thrilling measure;
At that cry each girl again
    Hugs her hidden treasure.

Round the middle of the grove
    Was a place enchanted,
Which the god for his own rites
    Specially had planted;
Fauns and nymphs and satyrs here
    Flowery alleys haunted,
And before the face of Love
    Played and leaped and chaunted.

In their hands they carry thyme,
    Crowns of fragrant roses;
Bacchus leads the choir divine
    And the dance composes;
Nymphs and fauns with feet in tune
    Interchange their posies;
But Silenus trips and reels
    When the chorus closes.

On an ass the elder borne
　　All the mad crew guideth ;
Mirth and laughter at the view
　　Through Love's glad heart glideth.
" Io ! " shouts the eld ; that sound
　　In his throat subsideth,
For his voice in wine is drowned,
　　And his old age chideth.

'Mid these pleasant sights appears
　　Love, the young joy-giver ;
Bright as stars his eyes, and wings
　　On his shoulders shiver ;
In his left hand is the bow,
　　At his side the quiver ;
From his state the world may know
　　He is lord for ever.

Leans the boy upon a staff
　　Intertwined with flowers,
Scent of nectar from his hair
　　Breathes around the bowers ;
Hand in hand before him kneel
　　Three celestial Hours,
Graces who Love's goblet fill
　　From immortal showers.

It would surely be superfluous to point out the fluent
elegance of this poem, or to dwell farther upon the
astonishing fact that anything so purely Renaissance in
tone should have been produced in the twelfth century.
　　Cupid, as was natural, settles the dispute of the two

girls by deciding that scholars are more suitable for love than soldiers.

This would be the place to introduce another long descriptive poem, if the nature of its theme rendered it fit for translation. It relates the visit of a student to what he calls the *Templum Veneris;* in other words, to the house of a courtesan. Her attendants are sirens; and the whole poem, dealing with a vulgar incident, is conducted in this mock-heroic strain.[1]

XVII

We pass now to love-poems of a more purely personal kind. One of these, which is too long for translation and in some respects ill-suited to a modern taste, forms the proper transition from the descriptive to the lyrical section. It starts with phrases culled from hymns to the Virgin :—

> "Si linguis angelicis
> Loquar et humanis."

> "Ave formosissima,
> Gemma pretiosa;
> Ave decus virginum,
> Virgo gloriosa!"

These waifs and strays of religious diction are curiously blent with romantic and classical allusions. The girl is addressed in the same breath as—

> "Blanziflor et Helena,
> Venus generosa."

Toward the close of the poem, the lover, who at

[1] *Carmina Burana*, p. 138.

length has reached the object of his heart's desire,
breaks into this paean of victorious passion :—

"What more ?   Around the maiden's neck
    My arms I flung with yearning;
Upon her lips I gave and took
    A thousand kisses burning :
Again and yet again I cried,
    With whispered vows and sighing,
This, this alone, sure, sure it was
    For which my heart was dying !

Who is the man that does not know
    The sweets that followed after ?
My former pains, my sobs and woe,
    Were changed for love and laughter :
The joys of Paradise were ours
    In overflowing measure ;
We tasted every shape of bliss
    And every form of pleasure."

The next piece which I shall quote differs in some
important respects from the general style adopted by
the Goliardi in their love-poetry. It is written in
rhyming or leonine hexameters, and is remarkable for
its quaint play on names, conceived and executed in a
truly medieval taste.

FLOS FLORAE

No. 30

TAKE thou this rose, O Rose ! the loves in the
    rose repose :
I with love of the rose am caught at the winter's close :

Take thou this flower, my flower, and cherish it in
    thy bower :
Thou in thy beauty's power shalt lovelier blow each
    hour :
Gaze at the rose, and smile, my rose, in mine eyes the
    while :
To thee the roses belong, thy voice is the nightingale's
    song :
Give thou the rose a kiss, it blushes like thy mouth's
    bliss :
Flowers in a picture seem not flowers, but flowers in a
    dream :
Who paints the rose's bloom, paints not the rose's
    perfume.

In complete contrast to this conceited and euphuistic
style of composition stands a slight snatch of rustic
melody, consisting of little but reiteration and refrain.

A BIRD'S SONG OF LOVE

No. 31

COME to me, O come !
Let me not die, but come !
    Hyria hysria nazaza
      Trillirivos.

Fair is thy face, O fair !
Fair thine eyes, O how fair !
    Hyria hysria nazaza
      Trillirivos.

Fair is thy flowing hair !
O fair, O fair, how fair !
          Hyria hysria nazaza
              Trillirivos.

Redder than rose art thou,
Whiter than lily thou !
          Hyria hysria nazaza
              Trillirivos.

Fairer than all, I vow,
Ever my pride art thou !
          Hyria hysria nazaza
              Trillirivos.

The following displays an almost classical intensity
of voluptuous passion, and belongs in all probability to a
period later than the *Carmina Burana*. I have ventured,
in translating it, to borrow the structure of a song which
occurs in Fletcher's *Rollo* (act v. scene 2), the first
stanza of which is also found in Shakespeare's *Measure
for Measure* (act iv. scene 1), and to insert one or two
phrases from Fletcher's version. Whether the composer
of that song had ever met with the Latin lyric to Lydia
can scarcely form the subject of critical conjecture. Yet
there is a faint evanescent resemblance between the two
poems.

TO LYDIA

No. 32

LYDIA bright, thou girl more white
   Than the milk of morning new,
Or young lilies in the light!
  Matched with thy rose-whiteness, hue
Of red rose or white rose pales,
And the polished ivory fails,
           Ivory fails.

Spread, O spread, my girl, thy hair,
   Amber-hued and heavenly bright,
As fine gold or golden air!
  Show, O show thy throat so white,
Throat and neck that marble fine
Over thy white breasts incline,
           Breasts incline.

Lift, O lift thine eyes that are
   Underneath those eyelids dark,
Lustrous as the evening star
   'Neath the dark heaven's purple arc!
Bare, O bare thy cheeks of rose,
Dyed with Tyrian red that glows,
           Red that glows.

Give, O give those lips of love
   That the coral boughs eclipse;
Give sweet kisses, dove by dove,
   Soft descending on my lips.

See my soul how forth she flies !
'Neath each kiss my pierced heart dies,
                    Pierced heart dies.

Wherefore dost thou draw my life,
    Drain my heart's blood with thy kiss ?
Scarce can I endure the strife
    Of this ecstasy of bliss !
Set, O set my poor heart free,
Bound in icy chains by thee,
                    Chains by thee.

Hide, O hide those hills of snow,
    Twinned upon thy breast that rise,
Where the virgin fountains flow
    With fresh milk of Paradise !
Thy bare bosom breathes of myrrh,
From thy whole self pleasures stir,
                    Pleasures stir.

Hide, O hide those paps that tire
    Sense and spirit with excess
Of snow-whiteness and desire
    Of thy breast's deliciousness !
See'st thou, cruel, how I swoon ?
Leav'st thou me half lost so soon ?
                    Lost so soon ?

In rendering this lyric to Lydia, I have restored the
fifth stanza, only one line of which,

      "Quid mihi sugis vivum sanguinem,"

remains in the original.   This I did because it seemed

necessary to effect the transition from the stanzas beginning *Pande, puella, pande,* to those beginning *Conde papillas, conde.*

Among these more direct outpourings of personal passion, place may be found for a delicate little *Poem of Privacy,* which forms part of the *Carmina Burana.* Unfortunately, the text of this slight piece is very defective in the MS., and has had to be conjecturally restored in several places.

A POEM OF PRIVACY

No. 33

WHEN a young man, passion-laden,
　　In a chamber meets a maiden,
Then felicitous communion,
By love's strain between the twain,
　　Grows from forth their union ;
For the game, it hath no name,
Of lips, arms, and hidden charms.

Nor can I here forbear from inserting another *Poem of Privacy,* bolder in its openness of speech, more glowing in its warmth of colouring. If excuse should be pleaded for the translation and reproduction of this distinctly Pagan ditty, it must be found in the singularity of its motive, which is as unmedieval as could be desired by the bitterest detractor of medieval sentiment. We seem, while reading it, to have before our eyes the Venetian picture of a Venus, while the almost prosaic

particularity of description illustrates what I have said
above about the detailed realism of the Goliardic
style.

FLORA

No. 34

RUDELY blows the winter blast,
    Withered leaves are falling fast,
Cold hath hushed the birds at last.
    While the heavens were warm and glowing,
        Nature's offspring loved in May ;
    But man's heart no debt is owing
        To such change of month or day
        As the dumb brute-beasts obey.
Oh, the joys of this possessing !
How unspeakable the blessing
        That my Flora yields to-day !

Labour long I did not rue,
Ere I won my wages due,
And the prize I played for drew.
    Flora with her brows of laughter,
        Gazing on me, breathing bliss,
    Draws my yearning spirit after,
        Sucks my soul forth in a kiss :
        Where's the pastime matched with this ?
Oh, the joys of this possessing !
How unspeakable the blessing
        Of my Flora's loveliness !

Truly mine is no harsh doom,
While in this secluded room
Venus lights for me the gloom!
   Flora faultless as a blossom
     Bares her smooth limbs for mine eyes;
   Softly shines her virgin bosom,
     And the breasts that gently rise
     Like the hills of Paradise.
Oh, the joys of this possessing!
How unspeakable the blessing
     When my Flora is the prize!

From her tender breasts decline,
In a gradual curving line,
Flanks like swansdown white and fine.
   On her skin the touch discerneth
     Naught of rough; 'tis soft as snow:
   'Neath the waist her belly turneth
     Unto fulness, where below
     In Love's garden lilies blow.
Oh, the joys of this possessing!
How unspeakable the blessing!
     Sweetest sweets from Flora flow!

Ah! should Jove but find my fair,
He would fall in love, I swear,
And to his old tricks repair:
   In a cloud of gold descending
     As on Danae's brazen tower,
   Or the sturdy bull's back bending,
     Or would veil his godhood's power
     In a swan's form for one hour.

> Oh, the joys of this possessing !
> How unspeakable the blessing !
> How divine my Flora's flower !

A third "poem of privacy" may be employed to temper this too fervid mood. I conceive it to be meant for the monologue of a lover in the presence of his sweetheart, and to express the varying lights and shades of his emotion.

THE LOVER'S MONOLOGUE

No. 35

LOVE rules everything that is :
Love doth change hearts in a kiss :
Love seeks devious ways of bliss :
   Love than honey sweeter,
   Love than gall more bitter.
Blind Love hath no modesties.
   Love is lukewarm, fiery, cold ;
   Love is timid, overbold ;
   Loyal, treacherous, manifold.

Present time is fit for play :
Let Love find his mate to-day :
Hark, the birds, how sweet their lay !
   Love rules young men wholly ;
   Love lures maidens solely.
Woe to old folk ! sad are they.
   Sweetest woman ever seen,
   Fairest, dearest, is my queen ;
   And alas ! my chiefest teen.

Let an old man, chill and drear,
Never come thy bosom near ;
 Oft he sleeps with sorry cheer,
       Too cold to delight thee :
       Naught could less invite thee.
Youth with youth must mate, my dear.
   Blest the union I desire ;
   Naught I know and naught require,
   Better than to be thy squire.

Love flies all the world around :
Love in wanton wiles is wound :
Therefore youth and maid are bound
       In Love's fetters duly.
       She is joyless truly
Who no lover yet hath found !
   All the night in grief and smart
   She must languish, wear her heart ;
   Bitter is that woman's part.

Love is simple, Love is sly ;
Love is pale, of ruddy dye :
Love is all things, low and high :
       Love is serviceable,
       Constant and unstable :
Love obeys Art's empery.
   In this closed room Love takes flight,
   In the silence of the night,
   Love made captive, conquered quite.

 The next is singularly, quaintly musical in the
original, but for various reasons I have not been able to

adhere exactly to its form.   I imagine that it is the
work of the same poet who composed the longer piece
which I shall give immediately after.   Both are
addressed to Caecilia; I have used the name Phyllis
in my version.

THE INVITATION TO LOVE

No. 36

L IST, my girl, with words I woo;
  Lay not wanton hands on you :
Sit before you, in your face
Gazing, ah ! and seeking grace:
Fix mine eyes, nor let them rove
From the mark where shafts of love
        Their flight wing.
Try, my girl, O try what bliss
Young men render when they kiss !

Youth is alway sturdy, straight ;
Old age totters in its gait.
These delights of love we bring
Have the suppleness of spring,
Softness, sweetness, wantoning ;
Clasp, my Phyllis, in their ring
Sweeter sweets than poets sing,
        Anything and everything !

After daytime's heat from heaven
Dews on thirsty fields are given ;
After verdant leaf and stem
Shoots the white flower's diadem ;

After the white flower's bloom
To the night their faint perfume
Lilies fling.
Try, my girl, etc., *da capo*.

The poem, *Ludo cum Caecilia*, which comes next in
order, is one of the most perfect specimens of Goliardic
writing.   To render its fluent, languid, and yet airy
grace, in any language but the Latin, is, I think, impossible.   Who could have imagined that the subtlety,
the refinement, almost the perversity of feeling expressed
in it, should have been proper to a student of the
twelfth century?   The poem is spoiled toward its
close by astrological and grammatical conceits; and
the text is corrupt.   That part I have omitted,
together with some stanzas which offend a modern
taste.

PHYLLIS

No. 37

THINK no evil, have no fear,
    If I play with Phyllis;
I am but the guardian dear
    Of her girlhood's lilies,
Lest too soon her bloom should swoon
    Like spring's daffodillies.

All I care for is to play,
    Gaze upon my treasure,
Now and then to touch her hand,
    Kiss in modest measure;

But the fifth act of love's game,
 Dream not of that pleasure !

For to touch the bloom of youth
 Spoils its frail complexion ;
Let the young grape gently grow
 Till it reach perfection ;
Hope within my heart doth glow
 Of the girl's affection.

Sweet above all sweets that are
 'Tis to play with Phyllis ;
For her thoughts are white as snow,
 In her heart no ill is ;
And the kisses that she gives
 Sweeter are than lilies.

Love leads after him the gods
 Bound in pliant traces ;
Harsh and stubborn hearts he bends,
 Breaks with blows of maces ;
Nay, the unicorn is tamed
 By a girl's embraces.

Love leads after him the gods,
 Jupiter with Juno ;
To his waxen measure treads
 Masterful Neptune O !
Pluto stern to souls below
 Melts to this one tune O !

Whatsoe'er the rest may do,
 Let us then be playing :

Take the pastime that is due
    While we're yet a-Maying;
I am young and young are you;
    'Tis the time for playing.

Up to this time, the happiness of love returned
and satisfied has been portrayed. The following lyric
exhibits a lover pining at a distance, soothing his soul
with song, and indulging in visions of happiness beyond
his grasp—εἰδώλοις κάλλευς κῶφα χλιαινόμενος, as
Meleager phrased it on a similar occasion.

LOVE LONGINGS

No. 38

WITH song I seek my fate to cheer,
    As doth the swan when death draws near;
Youth's roses from my cheeks retire,
My heart is worn with fond desire.
        Since care and woe increase and grow, while
            light burns low,
                Poor wretch I die!
        Heigho! I die, poor wretch I die!
Constrained to love, unloved; such luck have I!

If she could love me whom I love,
I would not then exchange with Jove:

Ah! might I clasp her once, and drain
Her lips as thirsty flowers drink rain!
    With death to meet, his welcome greet, from
       life retreat,
          I were full fain!
    Heigho! full fain, I were full fain,
Could I such joy, such wealth of pleasure gain!

When I bethought me of her breast,
Those hills of snow my fancy pressed;
Longing to touch them with my hand,
Love's laws I then did understand.
    Rose of the south, blooms on her mouth; I
       felt love's drouth
          That mouth to kiss!
    Heigho! to kiss, that mouth to kiss!
Lost in day-dreams and vain desires of bliss.

The next is the indignant repudiation by a lover
of the calumny that he has proved unfaithful to his
mistress. The strongly marked double rhymes of the
original add peculiar vehemence to his protestations;
while the abundance of cheap mythological allusions is
emphatically Goliardic.

THE LOVER'S VOW

No. 39

FALSE the tongue and foul with slander,
  Poisonous treacherous tongue of pander,
Tongue the hangman's knife should sever,
Tongue in flames to burn for ever;

Which hath called me a deceiver,
Faithless lover, quick to leave her,
Whom I love, and leave her slighted,
For another, unrequited !

Hear, ye Muses nine ! nay, rather,
Jove, of gods and men the father !
Who for Danae and Europa
Changed thy shape, thou bold eloper !

Hear me, god ! ye gods all, hear me !
Such a sin came never near me.
Hear, thou god ! and gods all, hear ye !
Thus I sinned not, as I fear ye.

I by Mars vow, by Apollo,
Both of whom Love's learning follow ;
Yea, by Cupid too, the terror
Of whose bow forbids all error !

By thy bow I vow and quiver,
By the shafts thou dost deliver,
Without fraud, in honour duly
To observe my troth-plight truly.

I will keep the troth I plighted,
And the reason shall be cited :
'Tis that 'mid the girls no maiden
Ever met I more love-laden.

'Mid the girls thou art beholden
Like a pearl in setting golden ;
Yea, thy shoulder, neck, and bosom
Bear of beauty's self the blossom.

Oh, her throat, lips, forehead, nourish
Love, with food that makes him flourish !
And her curls, I did adore them—
They were blonde with heaven's light o'er them.

Therefore, till, for Nature's scorning,
Toil is rest and midnight morning,
Till no trees in woods are growing,
Till fire turns to water flowing ;

Till seas have no ships to sail them,
Till the Parthians' arrows fail them,
I, my girl, will love thee ever,
Unbetrayed, betray thee never !

In the following poem a lover bids adieu for ever to
an unworthy woman, who has betrayed him.   This is
a remarkable specimen of the songs written for a
complicated melody.   The first eight lines seem set
to one tune ; in the next four that tune is slightly
accelerated, and a double rhyme is substituted for a
single one in the tenth and twelfth verses.   The five
concluding lines go to a different kind of melody, and
express in each stanza a changed mood of feeling.

I have tried in this instance to adopt the plaster-cast
method of translation, as described above,[1] and have
even endeavoured to obtain the dragging effect of the
first eight lines of each strophe, which are composed
neither of exact accentual dactyls nor yet of exact
accentual anapaests, but offer a good example of that
laxity of rhythm permitted in this prosody for music.

[1] Page 37.

Comparison with the original will show that I was not copying Byron's *When we Two Parted ;* yet the resemblance between that song and the tone which my translation has naturally assumed from the Latin, is certainly noticeable. That Byron could have seen the piece before he wrote his own lines in question is almost impossible, for this portion of the *Carmina Burana* had not, so far as I am aware, been edited before the year 1847. The coincidence of metrical form, so far as it extends, only establishes the spontaneity of emotion which, in the case of the medieval and the modern poet, found a similar rhythm for the utterance of similar feeling.

FAREWELL TO THE FAITHLESS

No. 40

A MORTAL anguish
    How often woundeth me ;
Grieving I languish,
    Weighed down with misery ;
Hearing the mournful
    Tale of thy fault and fall
Blown by Fame's scornful
    Trump to the ears of all !

Envious rumour
    Late or soon will slay thee :
Love with less humour,
    Lest thy love betray thee.

Whate'er thou dost, do secretly,
Far from Fame's curiosity;
Love in the dark delights to be,
His sports are wiles and witchery,
    With laugh of lovers greeting.

Thou wert not slighted,
    Stained in thine honour, when
We were united,
    Lovers unknown to men;
But when thy passion
    Grew like thy bosom cold,
None had compassion,
    Then was thy story told.

Fame, who rejoiceth
    New amours to utter,
Now thy shame voiceth,
    Wide her pinions flutter.

The palace home of modesty
Is made a haunt for harlotry;
The virgin lily you may see
Defiled by fingers lewd and free,
    With vile embraces meeting.

I mourn the tender
    Flower of the youth of thee,
Brighter in splendour
    Than evening's star can be.

Pure were thy kisses,
    Dove-like thy smile;
As the snake hisses
    Now is thy guile.

Lovers who pray thee
  From thy door are scattered ;
Lovers who pay thee
  In thy bed are flattered.

Thou bidst them from thy presence flee
From whom thou canst not take thy fee ;
Blind, halt, and lame thy suitors be ;
Illustrious men with subtlety
  And poisonous honey cheating.

I may add that a long soliloquy printed in *Carmina Burana*, pp. 119–121, should be compared with the foregoing lyric. It has a similar motive, though the lover in this case expresses his willingness for reconciliation. One part of its expostulation with the faithless woman is beautiful in its simplicity :—

" Amaveram prae caeteris
  Te, sed amici veteris
  Es jam oblita ! Superis
  Vel inferis
  Ream te criminamur."

I will close this section with the lament written for a medieval Gretchen whose fault has been discovered, and whose lover has been forced to leave the country. Its bare realism contrasts with the lyrical exuberance of the preceding specimens.

GRETCHEN

No. 41

UP to this time, well-away!
   I concealed the truth from day,
   Went on loving skilfully.
Now my fault at length is clear :
That the hour of need is near,
   From my shape all eyes can see.
So my mother gives me blows,
So my father curses throws ;
   They both treat me savagely.
In the house alone I sit,
Dare not walk about the street,
   Nor at play in public be.

If I walk about the street,
Every one I chance to meet
   Scans me like a prodigy :
When they see the load I bear,
All the neighbours nudge and stare,
   Gaping while I hasten by ;
With their elbows nudge, and so
With their finger point, as though
   I were some monstrosity ;
Me with nods and winks they spurn,
Judge me fit in flames to burn
   For one lapse from honesty.

Why this tedious tale prolong?
Short, I am become a song,
  In all mouths a mockery.
By this am I done to death,
Sorrow kills me, chokes my breath,
  Ever weep I bitterly.
One thing makes me still more grieve,
That my friend his home must leave
  For the same cause instantly ;
Therefore is my sadness so
Multiplied, weighed down with woe,
  For he too will part from me.

XVIII

A separate section should be assigned to poems of
exile.   They are not very numerous, but are interesting in connection with the wandering life of their
vagrant authors.   The first has all the dreamy pathos
felt by a young German leaving his beloved home in
some valley of the Suabian or Thuringian hills.

ADIEU TO THE VALLEY

No. 42

OH, of love twin-brother anguish !
  In thy pangs I faint and languish,
    Cannot find relief from thee !
Nay, no marvel !   I must grieve her,
Wander forth in exile, leave her,
    Who hath gained the heart of me ;

Who of loveliness so rare is
That for her sake Trojan Paris
  Would have left his Helenë.

Smile, thou valley, sweetest, fairest,
Wreathed with roses of the rarest,
  Flower of all the vales that be !
Vale of vales, all vales excelling,
Sun and moon thy praise are telling,
  With the song-birds' melody ;
Nightingales thy praise are singing,
O thou soothing solace-bringing
  To the soul's despondency !

The second was probably intended to be sung at a
drinking-party by a student taking leave of his com-
panions. It is love that forces him to quit their
society and to break with his studies. The long
rhyming lines, followed by a sharp drop at the close of
each stanza upon a short disjointed phrase, seem to
indicate discouragement and melancholy.

THE LOVER'S PARTING

No. 43

SWEET native soil, farewell ! dear country of
    my birth !
Fair chamber of the loves ! glad home of joy and
    mirth !

To-morrow or to-day I leave you, o'er the earth
To wander struck with love, to pine with rage and
dearth
> In exile !

Farewell, sweet land, and ye, my comrades dear,
adieu !
To whom with kindly heart I have been ever true ;
The studies that we loved I may no more pursue ;
Weep then for me, who part as though I died to you,
> Love-laden !

As many as the flowers that Hybla's valley cover,
As many as the leaves that on Dodona hover,
As many as the fish that sail the wide seas over,
So many are the pangs that pain a faithful lover,
> For ever !

With the new fire of love my wounded bosom burns ;
Love knows not any ruth, all tender pity spurns ;
How true the proverb speaks that saith to him that
yearns,
" Where love is there is pain ; thy pleasure love
returns
> With anguish ! "

Ah, sorrow ! ah, how sad the wages of our bliss !
In lovers' hearts the flame's too hot for happiness ;
For Venus still doth send new sighs and new distress
When once the enamoured soul is taken with excess
> Of sweetness !

The third introduces us to a little episode of medieval private life which must have been frequent enough.
It consists of a debate between a father and his son
upon the question whether the young man should enter
into a monastic brotherhood.   The youth is lying on
a sickbed, and thinks that he is already at the point of
death.   It will be noticed that he is only diverted
from his project by the mention of a student friend
(indicated, as usual, by an N), whom he would never
be able to see again if he assumed the cowl.   I suspect,
however, that the poem has not been transmitted to
us entire.

IN ARTICULO MORTIS

No. 44

Son.   OH, my father ! help, I pray !
　　　　Death is near my soul to-day ;
　　　With your blessing let me be
　　　Made a monk right speedily !

　　　See the foe my life invade !
　　　Haste, oh haste, to give me aid !
　　　Bring me comfort and heart's ease,
　　　Strengthen me in this disease !

Father. Oh, my best-belovèd son,
　　　　What is this thou wouldst have done ?
　　　Weigh it well in heart and brain :
　　　Do not leave me here in pain.

Son. Father, this thy loving care
  Makes me weep full sore, I swear ;
  For you will be childless when
  I have joined those holy men.

Father. Therefore make a little stay,
  Put it off till the third day ;
  It may be your danger is
  Not unto the death, I wis.

Son. Such the anguish that I feel
  Through my inmost entrails steal,
  That I bide in doubt lest death
  Ere to-morrow end my breath.

Father. Those strict rules that monks observe,
  Well I know them !   They must serve
  Heaven by fasting every day,
  And by keeping watch alway.

Son. Who for God watch through the night
  Shall receive a crown of light ;
  Who for heaven's sake hungers, he
  Shall be fed abundantly.

Father. Hard and coarse the food they eat,
  Beans and pottage-herbs their meat ;
  After such a banquet, think,
  Water is their only drink !

Son. What's the good of feasts, or bright
  Cups of Bacchus, when, in spite
  Of all comforts, at the last
  This poor flesh to worms is cast ?

Father. Well, then, let thy parent's moan
    Move thee in thy soul, my son !
    Mourning for thee made a monk,
    Dead-alive in darkness sunk.

Son. They who father, mother love,
    And their God neglect, will prove
    That they are in error found
    When the judgment trump shall sound.

Father. Logic ! would thou ne'er hadst been
    Known on earth for mortal teen !
    Many a clerk thou mak'st to roam
    Wretched, exiled from his home.—

    Never more thine eyes, my son,
    Shall behold thy darling one,
    Him, that little clerk so fair,
    N., thy friend beyond compare !

Son. Oh, alas ! unhappy me !
    What to do I cannot see ;
    Wandering lost in exile so,
    Without guide or light I go !—

    Dry your tears, my father dear,
    Haply there is better cheer ;
    Now my mind on change is set,
    I'll not be a monk, not yet.

XIX

The order adopted in this essay brings us now to
drinking-songs.   Next to spring and love, our students

set their affections principally on the tavern and the wine-
bowl.   In the poems on the Order we have seen how
large a space in their vagrant lives was occupied by the
tavern and its jovial company of topers and gamesters.
It was there that—

> "Some are gaming, some are drinking,
> Some are living without thinking ;
> And of those who make the racket,
> Some are stripped of coat and jacket ;
> Some get clothes of finer feather,
> Some are cleaned out altogether ;
> No one there dreads death's invasion,
> But all drink in emulation."

The song from which I have extracted this stanza
contains a parody of S. Thomas Aquinas' hymn on the
Eucharist.[1]   To translate it seemed to me impossible;
but I will cite the following stanza, which may be
compared with stanzas ix. and x. of *Lauda Sion* :—

> "Bibit hera, bibit herus,
> Bibit miles, bibit clerus,
> Bibit ille, bibit illa,
> Bibit servus cum ancilla,
> Bibit velox, bibit piger,
> Bibit albus, bibit niger,
> Bibit constans, bibit vagus,
> Bibit rudis, bibit magus."

Several of the best anacreontics of the period are
even more distinctly parodies.   The following panegyric
of wine, for example, is modelled upon a hymn to the
Virgin :—

[1] *In Taberna, Carm. Bur.*, p. 235.

A SEQUENCE IN PRAISE OF WINE

No. 45

WINE the good and bland, thou blessing
　　Of the good, the bad's distressing,
Sweet of taste by all confessing,
　　Hail, thou world's felicity !
Hail thy hue, life's gloom dispelling ;
Hail thy taste, all tastes excelling ;
By thy power, in this thy dwelling
　　Deign to make us drunk with thee !

Oh, how blest for bounteous uses
Is the birth of pure vine-juices !
Safe's the table which produces
　　Wine in goodly quality.
Oh, in colour how auspicious !
Oh, in odour how delicious !
In the mouth how sweet, propitious
　　To the tongue enthralled by thee !

Blest the man who first thee planted,
Called thee by thy name enchanted !
He whose cups have ne'er been scanted
　　Dreads no danger that may be.
Blest the belly where thou bidest !
Blest the tongue where thou residest !
Blest the mouth through which thou glidest,
　　And the lips thrice blest by thee !

Therefore let wine's praise be sounded,
Healths to topers all propounded ;
We shall never be confounded,
　　Toping for eternity !
Pray we : here be thou still flowing,
Plenty on our board bestowing,
While with jocund voice we're showing
　　How we serve thee—Jubilee !

Another, regarding the date of which I have no information, is an imitation of a well-known *Christmas Carol.*

A CAROL OF WINE

No. 46

IN dulci jubilo
Sing we, make merry so !
　　Since our heart's pleasure
Latet in poculo,
　　Drawn from the cask, good measure,
Pro hoc convivio,
　　　Nunc, nunc bibito !

O crater parvule !
How my soul yearns for thee !
　　Make me now merry,
O potus optime,
　　Claret or hock or sherry !
Et vos concinite :
　　　Vivant socii !

O vini caritas!
O Bacchi lenitas!
  We've drained our purses
Per multa pocula:
  Yet hope we for new mercies,
Nummorum gaudia:
    Would that we had them, ah!

Ubi sunt gaudia? where,
If that they be not there?
  There the lads are singing
Selecta cantica:
  There are glasses ringing
In villae curia;
    Oh, would that we were there!

In Dulci Jubilo yields an example of mixed Latin
and German. This is the case too with a comparatively ancient drinking-song quoted by Geiger in his
Renaissance und Humanismus, p. 414. It may be
mentioned that the word *Bursae*, for *Burschen*, occurs
in stanza v. This word, to indicate a student, can
also be found in *Carm. Bur.*, p. 236, where we are
introduced to scholars drinking yellow Rhine wine out
of glasses of a pale pink colour—already in the twelfth
century!

THE STUDENTS' WINE-BOUT

No. 47

HO, all ye jovial brotherhood,
　　Quos sitis vexat plurima,
I know a host whose wits are good,
　　Quod vina spectat optima.

His wine he blends not with the juice
　　E puteo qui sumitur ;
Each kind its virtue doth produce
　　E botris ut exprimitur.

Host, bring us forth good wine and strong,
　　In cella quod est optimum !
We brethren will our sport prolong
　　Ad noctis usque terminum.

Whoso to snarl or bite is fain,
　　Ut canes decet rabidos,
Outside our circle may remain,
　　Ad porcos eat sordidos.

Hurrah ! my lads, we'll merry make !
　　Levate sursum pocula !
God's blessing on all wine we take,
　　In sempiterna saecula !

Two lyrics of distinguished excellence, which still
hold their place in the *Commersbuch*, cannot claim
certain antiquity in their present form. They are not
included in the *Carmina Burana* ; yet their style is so

characteristic of the Archipoeta, that I believe we may
credit him with at least a share in their composition.
The first starts with an allusion to the Horatian *tempus
edax rerum.*

TIME'S A-FLYING

No. 48

LAUREL-CROWNED Horatius,
     True, how true thy saying!
Swift as wind flies over us
     Time, devouring, slaying.
Where are, oh! those goblets full
     Of wine honey-laden,
Strifes and loves and bountiful
     Lips of ruddy maiden?

Grows the young grape tenderly,
     And the maid is growing;
But the thirsty poet, see,
     Years on him are snowing!
What's the use on hoary curls
     Of the bays undying,
If we may not kiss the girls,
     Drink while time's a-flying?

The second consists of a truly brilliant development
of the theme which our Herrick condensed into one
splendid phrase—"There's no lust like to poetry!"

THERE'S NO LUST LIKE TO POETRY

No. 49

SWEET in goodly fellowship
  Tastes red wine and rare O!
But to kiss a girl's ripe lip
  Is a gift more fair O!
Yet a gift more sweet, more fine,
  Is the lyre of Maro!
While these three good gifts were mine,
  I'd not change with Pharaoh.

Bacchus wakes within my breast
  Love and love's desire,
Venus comes and stirs the blessed
  Rage of Phœbus' fire;
Deathless honour is our due
  From the laurelled sire:
Woe should I turn traitor to
  Wine and love and lyre!

Should a tyrant rise and say,
  " Give up wine! " I'd do it;
" Love no girls! " I would obey,
  Though my heart should rue it.
" Dash thy lyre! " suppose he saith,
  Naught should bring me to it;
" Yield thy lyre or die! " my breath,
  Dying, should thrill through it!

A lyric of the elder period in praise of wine and
love, which forcibly illustrates the contempt felt by the

student class for the unlettered laity and boors, shall be
inserted here.   It seems to demand a tune.

WINE AND VENUS

No. 50

HO, comrades mine !
    What is your pleasure ?
What business fine
    Or mirthful measure ?
Lo, Venus toward our crew advancing,
A choir of Dryads round her dancing !

    Good fellows you !
        The time is jolly !
    Earth springs anew,
        Bans melancholy ;
Bid long farewell to winter weather !
Let lads and maids be blithe together.

    Dame Venus spurns
        Her brother Ocean ;
    To Bacchus turns ;
        No colder potion
Deserves her godhead's approbation ;
On sober souls she pours damnation.

    Let then this band,
        Imbued with learning,
    By Venus stand,
        Her wages earning !
Laymen we spurn from our alliance,
Like brutes to art deaf, dumb to science.

WINE AND VENUS

> Two gods alone
>> We serve and mate with ;
> One law we own,
>> Nor hold debate with :
> Who lives the goodly student fashion
> Must love and win love back with passion !

Among drinking-songs of the best period in this literature may be reckoned two disputations between water and wine. In the one, Thetis defends herself against Lyaeus, and the poet assists in vision at their contest. The scene is appropriately laid in the third sphere, the pleasant heaven of Venus. The other, which on the whole appears to me preferable, and which I have therefore chosen for translation, begins and ends with the sound axiom that water and wine ought never to be mixed. It is manifest that the poet reserves the honour of the day for wine, though his arguments are fair to both sides. The final point, which breaks the case of water down and determines her utter confusion, is curious, since it shows that people in the Middle Ages were fully alive to the perils of sewage-contaminated wells.

THE CONTEST OF WINE AND WATER

No. 51

LAYING truth bare, stripped of fable.
Briefly as I may be able,
With good reasons manifold,

I will tell why man should never
Copulate, but rather sever,
 Things that strife and hatred hold.

When one cup in fell confusion
Wine with water blends, the fusion,
 Call it by what name you will,
Is no blessing, nor deserveth
Any praise, but rather serveth
 For the emblem of all ill.

Wine perceives the water present,
And with pain exclaims, " What peasant
 Dared to mingle thee with me ?
Rise, go forth, get out, and leave me !
In the same place, here to grieve me,
 Thou hast no just claim to be.

" Vile and shameless in thy going,
Into cracks thou still art flowing,
 That in foul holes thou mayst lie ;
O'er the earth thou ought'st to wander,
On the earth thy liquor squander,
 And at length in anguish die.

" How canst thou adorn a table ?
No one sings or tells a fable
 In thy presence dull and drear ;
But the guest who erst was jolly,
Laughing, joking, bent on folly,
 Silent sits when thou art near.

" Should one drink of thee to fulness,
Sound before, he takes an illness ;
 All his bowels thou dost stir ;

Booms the belly, wind ariseth,
Which, enclosed and pent, surpriseth
  With a thousand sighs the ear.

" When the stomach's so inflated,
Blasts are then ejaculated
  From both draughts with divers sound ;
And that organ thus affected,
All the air is soon infected
  By the poison breathed around."

Water thus wine's home-thrust warded :
" All thy life is foul and sordid,
  Sunk in misery, steeped in vice ;
Those who drink thee lose their morals,
Waste their time in sloth and quarrels,
  Rolling down sin's precipice.

" Thou dost teach man's tongue to stutter ;
He goes reeling in the gutter
  Who hath deigned to kiss thy lips ;
Hears men speak without discerning,
Sees a hundred tapers burning
  When there are but two poor dips.

" He who feels for thee soul's hunger
Is a murderer or whoremonger,
  Davus Geta Birria ;
Such are they whom thou dost nourish ;
With thy fame and name they flourish
  In the tavern's disarray.

" Thou by reason of thy badness
Art confined in prison sadness,
  Cramped and small thy dwellings are :

I am great the whole world over,
Spread myself abroad and cover
   Every part of earth afar.

"Drink I yield to palates burning;
They who for soul's health are yearning,
   Need the aid that I have given;
Since all pilgrims, at their praying,
Far or near, I am conveying
   To the palaces of heaven."

Wine replied: "What thou hast vaunted
Proves thee full of fraud; for granted
   That thou carriest ships o'er sea,
Yet thou then dost swell and riot;
Till they wreck thou hast no quiet;
   Thus they are deceived through thee.

"He whose strength is insufficient
Thee to slake with heat efficient,
   Sunk in mortal peril lies:
Trusting thee the poor wretch waneth,
And through thee at length attaineth
   To the joys of Paradise.

"I'm a god, as that true poet
Naso testifies; men owe it
   Unto me that they are sage;
When they do not drink, professors
Lose their wits and lack assessors
   Round about the lecture-stage.

"'Tis impossible to sever
Truth from falsehood if you never
   Learn to drink my juices neat.

Thanks to me, dumb speak, deaf listen,
Blind folk see, the senses glisten,
   And the lame man finds his feet.

" Eld through me to youth returneth,
While thine influence o'erturneth
   All a young man's lustihead ;
By my force the world is laden
With new births, but boy or maiden
   Through thy help was never bred."

Water saith : " A god thou !   Just men
By thy craft become unjust men,
   Bad, worse, worst, degenerous !
Thanks to thee, their words half uttered
Through the drunken lips are stuttered,
   And thy sage is Didymus.

" I will speak the truth out wholly :
Earth bears fruit by my gift solely,
   And the meadows bloom in May ;
When it rains not, herbs and grasses
Dry with drought, spring's beauty passes,
   Flowers and lilies fade away.

" Lo, thy crookèd mother pining,
On her boughs the grapes declining,
   Barren through the dearth of rain ;
Mark her tendrils lean and sterile
O'er the parched earth at their peril
   Bent in unavailing pain !

" Famine through all lands prevaileth,
Terror-struck the people waileth,
   When I choose to keep away ;

Christians kneel to Christ to gain me,
Jews and Pagans to obtain me
   Ceaseless vows and offerings pay."

Wine saith : " To the deaf thou'rt singing
Those vain self-laudations flinging !
   Otherwhere thou hast been shown !
Patent 'tis to all the races
How impure and foul thy place is ;
   We believe what we have known !

" Thou of things the scum and rotten
Sewer, where ordures best forgotten
   And unmentioned still descend !
Filth and garbage, stench and poison,
Thou dost bear in fetid foison !
   Here I stop lest words offend."

Water rose, the foe invaded,
In her own defence upbraided
   Wine for his invective base :
" Now at last we've drawn the curtain !
Who, what god thou art is certain
   From thy oracle's disgrace.

" This thine impudent oration
Hurts not me ; 'tis desecration
   To a god, and fouls his tongue !
At the utmost at nine paces
Can I suffer filthy places,
   Fling far from me dirt and dung ! "

Wine saith : " This repudiation
Of my well-weighed imputation
   Doth not clear thyself of crime !

Many a man and oft who swallowed
Thine infected potion, followed
   After death in one day's time."

Hearing this, in stupefaction
Water stood ; no words, no action,
   Now restrained her sobs of woe.
Wine exclaims, " Why art thou dumb then ?
Without answer ? Is it come then
   To thy complete overthrow ? "

I who heard the whole contention
Now declare my song's intention,
   And to all the world proclaim :
They who mix these things shall ever
Henceforth be accursed, and never
   In Christ's kingdom portion claim.

The same precept, " Keep wine and water apart,"
is conveyed at the close of a lyric distinguished in
other respects for the brutal passion of its drunken
fervour. I have not succeeded in catching the rollick-
ing swing of the original verse ; and I may observe
that the last two stanzas seem to form a separate song,
although their metre is the same as that of the first
four.

BACCHIC FRENZY

No. 52

TOPERS in and out of season !
   'Tis not thirst but better reason
Bids you tope on steadily !—
Pass the wine-cup, let it be

Filled and filled for bout on bout !
Never sleep !
Racy jest and song flash out!
Spirits leap !

Those who cannot drink their rations,
Go, begone from these ovations !
Here's no place for bashful boys ;
Like the plague, they spoil our joys.—
Bashful eyes bring rustic cheer
When we're drunk,
And a blush betrays a drear
Want of spunk.

If there's here a fellow lurking
Who his proper share is shirking,
Let the door to him be shown,
From our crew we'll have him thrown ;—
He's more desolate than death,
Mixed with us ;
Let him go and end his breath !
Better thus !

When your heart is set on drinking,
Drink on without stay or thinking,
Till you cannot stand up straight,
Nor one word articulate !—
But herewith I pledge to you
This fair health :
May the glass no mischief do,
Bring you wealth !

Wed not you the god and goddess,
For the god doth scorn the goddess;
   He whose name is Liber, he
   Glories in his liberty.
   All her virtue in the cup
      Runs to waste,
   And wine wedded yieldeth up
      Strength and taste.

Since she is the queen of ocean,
Goddess she may claim devotion:
   But she is no mate to kiss
   His superior holiness.
   Bacchus never deigned to be
      Watered, he!
   Liber never bore to be
      Christened, he!

XX

Closely allied to drinking-songs are some comic ditties which may have been sung at wine-parties. Of these I have thought it worth while to present a few specimens, though their medieval bluntness of humour does not render them particularly entertaining to a modern reader.

The first I have chosen is *The Lament of the Roast Swan*. It must be remembered that this bird was esteemed a delicacy in the Middle Ages, and also that pepper was highly prized for its rarity. This gives a certain point to the allusion in the third stanza.

THE LAMENT OF THE ROAST SWAN

No. 53

TIME was my wings were my delight,
Time was I made a lovely sight;
'Twas when I was a swan snow-white.
Woe's me! I vow,
Black am I now,
Burned up, back, beak, and brow!

The baster turns me on the spit,
The fire I've felt the force of it,
The carver carves me bit by bit.

I'd rather in the water float
Under the bare heavens like a boat,
Than have this pepper down my throat.

Whiter I was than wool or snow,
Fairer than any bird I know;
Now am I blacker than a crow.

Now in the gravy-dish I lie,
I cannot swim, I cannot fly,
Nothing but gnashing teeth I spy.
Woe's me! I vow, &c.

The next is *The Last Will of the Dying Ass*.   There
is not much to be said for the wit of this piece.

THE WILL OF THE DYING ASS

No. 54

WHILE a boor, as poets tell,
  Whacked his patient ass too well,
On the ground half dead it fell.
  La sol fa,
On the ground half dead it fell,
  La sol fa mi re ut.

Then with gesture sad and low,
Streaming eyes and words of woe,
He at length addressed it so :

" Had I known, my gentle ass,
Thou from me so soon wouldst pass,
I'd have swaddled thee, alas !

" Made for thee a tunic meet,
Shirt and undershirt complete,
Breeches, drawers of linen sweet.

" Rise awhile, for pity's sake,
That ere life your limbs forsake
You your legacies may make ! "

Soon the ass stood up, and thus,
With a weak voice dolorous,
His last will proclaimed for us :

" To the magistrates my head,
Eyes to constables," he said,
" Ears to judges, when I'm dead ;

" To old men my teeth shall fall,
Lips to wanton wooers all,
And my tongue to wives that brawl.

" Let my feet the bailiffs win,
Nostrils the tobacco-men,
And fat canons take my skin.

" Voice to singing boys I give,
Throat to topers, may they live !
**** to students amative.

*** on shepherds I bestow,
Thistles on divines, and lo !
To the law my shade shall go.

" Elders have my tardy pace,
Boys my rude and rustic grace,
Monks my simple open face."

He who saith this testament
Will not hold, let him be shent ;
He's an ass by all consent.
La sol fa,
He's an ass by all consent,
La sol fa mi re ut.

As a third specimen I select a little bit of mixed
prose and verse from the *Carmina Burana,* which is
curious from its allusion to the Land of Cockaigne.
Goliardic literature, it may be parenthetically observed,
has some strong pieces of prose comedy and satire.
Of these, the *Mass of Topers* and *Mass of Gamesters,*
the *Gospel according to Marks,* and the description of a

IN THE SECT OF DECIUS

fat monk's daily life deserve quotation.[1] They are for the most part, however, too profane to bear translation.

THE ABBOT OF COCKAIGNE

No. 55

I AM the Abbot of Cockaigne,
  And this is my counsel with topers;
And in the sect of Decius (gamesters) this is my will;
And whoso shall seek me in taverns before noon;
After evensong shall he go forth naked,
And thus, stripped of raiment, shall lament him:
      Wafna! wafna!
    O Fate most foul, what hast thou done?
    The joys of man beneath the sun
    Thou hast stolen, every one!

XXI

The transition from these trivial and slightly interesting comic songs to poems of a serious import, which played so important a part in Goliardic literature, must of necessity be abrupt. It forms no part of my present purpose to exhibit the Wandering Students in their capacity as satirists. That belongs more properly to a study of the earlier Reformation than to such an inquiry as I have undertaken in this treatise. Satires,

[1] Wright's *Rel. Ant.*, ii.; *Carm. Bur.*, pp. 248 and 22; Wright's *Mapes*, p. xl.

especially medieval satires, are apt, besides, to lose
their force and value in translation.   I have therefore
confined myself to five specimens, more or less closely
connected with the subjects handled in this study.

The first has the interest of containing some ideas
which Villon preserved in his ballad of the men of old
time.

DEATH TAKES ALL

No. 56

HEAR, O thou earth, hear, thou encircling sea,
   Yea, all that live beneath the sun, hear ye
How of this world the bravery and the glory
Are but vain forms and shadows transitory,
Even as all things 'neath Time's empire show
By their short durance and swift overthrow !
   Nothing avails the dignity of kings,
Naught, naught avail the strength and stuff of things ;
The wisdom of the arts no succour brings ;
Genus and species help not at death's hour,
No man was saved by gold in that dread stour ;
The substance of things fadeth as a flower,
As ice 'neath sunshine melts into a shower.
   Where is Plato, where is Porphyrius ?
Where is Tullius, where is Virgilius ?
Where is Thales, where is Empedocles,
Or illustrious Aristoteles ?
Where's Alexander, peerless of might ?
Where is Hector, Troy's stoutest knight ?

Where is King David, learning's light?
Solomon where, that wisest wight?
Where is Helen, and Paris rose-bright?
 They have fallen to the bottom, as a stone rolls :
Who knows if rest be granted to their souls?
 But Thou, O God, of faithful men the Lord,
To us Thy favour evermore afford
When on the wicked judgment shall be poured !

The second marks the passage from those feelings
of youth and springtime which have been copiously
illustrated in Sections xiv.–xvii., to emotions befitting
later manhood and life's autumn.

AUTUMN YEARS

No. 57

WHILE life's April blossom blew,
 What I willed I then might do,
Lust and law seemed comrades true.
  As I listed, unresisted,
Hither, thither, could I play,
And my wanton flesh obey.

When life's autumn days decline,
Thus to live, a libertine,
Fancy-free as thoughts incline,
  Manhood's older age and colder
Now forbids ; removes, destroys
All those ways of wonted joys.

Age with admonition wise
Thus doth counsel and advise,
While her voice within me cries :
            " For repenting and relenting
There is room ; forgiveness falls
On all contrite prodigals ! "

I will seek a better mind ;
Change, correct, and leave behind
What I did with purpose blind :
            From vice sever, with endeavour
Yield my soul to serious things,
Seek the joy that virtue brings.

The third would find a more appropriate place in a
hymn-book than in a collection of *Carmina Vagorum*.
It is, however, written in a lyrical style so closely
allied to the secular songs of the *Carmina Burana*
(where it occurs) that I have thought it well to quote
its grimly medieval condemnation of human life.

VANITAS VANITATUM

No. 58

THIS vile world
    In madness hurled
        Offers but false shadows ;
Joys that wane
And waste like vain
        Lilies of the meadows.

Worldly wealth,
Youth, strength, and health,
    Cramp the soul's endeavour ;
Drive it down
In hell to drown,
    Hell that burns for ever.

What we see,
And what let be,
    While on earth we tarry,
We shall cast
Like leaves at last
    Which the sere oaks carry.

Carnal life,
Man's law of strife,
    Hath but brief existence;
Passes, fades,
Like wavering shades
    Without real subsistence.

Therefore bind,
Tread down and grind
    Fleshly lusts that blight us ;
So heaven's bliss
'Mid saints that kiss
    Shall for aye delight us.

The fourth, in like manner, would have but little
to do with a Commersbuch, were it not for the fact
that the most widely famous modern student-song of
Germany has borrowed two passages from its serious

and tragic rhythm.   Close inspection of *Gaudeamus Igitur* shows that the metrical structure of that song is based on the principle of quoting one of its long lines and rhyming to it.

ON CONTEMPT FOR THE WORLD

No. 59

" DE contemptu mundi : " this is the theme I've
      taken :
Time it is from sleep to rise, from death's torpor
      waken :
Gather virtue's grain and leave tares of sin forsaken.
      Rise up, rise, be vigilant; trim your lamp, be
      ready.

Brief is life, and brevity briefly shall be ended :
Death comes quick, fears no man, none hath his dart
      suspended :
Death kills all, to no man's prayer hath he con-
      descended.
      Rise up, rise, be vigilant; trim your lamp, be
      ready.

Where are they who in this world, ere we kept, were
      keeping ?
Come unto the churchyard, thou ! see where they are
      sleeping !
Dust and ashes are they, worms in their flesh are
      creeping.
      Rise up, rise, be vigilant; trim your lamp, be
      ready.

Into life each man is born with great teen and trouble :
All through life he drags along ; toil on toil is double :
When life's done, the pangs of death take him, break
  the bubble.
 Rise up, rise, be vigilant ; trim your lamp, be
  ready.

If from sin thou hast been turned, born a new man
  wholly,
Changed thy life to better things, childlike, simple,
  holy ;
Thus into God's realm shalt thou enter with the
  lowly.
 Rise up, rise, be vigilant ; trim your lamp, be
  ready.

 Having alluded to *Gaudeamus Igitur*, I shall close
my translations with a version of it into English. The
dependence of this lyric upon the rhythm and substance
of the poem on *Contempt for the World*, which I have
already indicated, is perhaps the reason why it is sung
by German students after the funeral of a comrade.
The Office for the Dead sounding in their ears,
occasions the startling *igitur* with which it opens ; and
their mind reverts to solemn phrases in the midst of
masculine determination to enjoy the present while it is
yet theirs.

GAUDEAMUS IGITUR

No. 60

LET us live, then, and be glad
  While young life's before us !
      After youthful pastime had,
      After old age hard and sad,
  Earth will slumber o'er us.

Where are they who in this world,
  Ere we kept, were keeping ?
      Go ye to the gods above ;
      Go to hell; inquire thereof :
  They are not ; they're sleeping.

Brief is life, and brevity
  Briefly shall be ended :
      Death comes like a whirlwind strong,
      Bears us with his blast along ;
  None shall be defended.

Live this university,
  Men that learning nourish ;
      Live each member of the same,
      Long live all that bear its name ;
  Let them ever flourish !

Live the commonwealth also,
  And the men that guide it !
      Live our town in strength and health,
      Founders, patrons, by whose wealth
  We are here provided !

Live all girls ! A health to you,
   Melting maids and beauteous !
      Live the wives and women too,
      Gentle, loving, tender, true,
   Good, industrious, duteous !

Perish cares that pule and pine !
   Perish envious blamers !
      Die the Devil, thine and mine !
      Die the starch-necked Philistine !
   Scoffers and defamers !

XXII

I have now fulfilled the purpose which I had in
view when I began this study of the *Carmina Vagorum*,
and have reproduced in English verse what seemed to
me the most characteristic specimens of that literature,
in so far as it may be considered precursory of the
Renaissance.

In spite of novelty, in spite of historical interest,
in spite of a certain literary charm, it is not an edify-
ing product of medieval art with which I have been
dealing. When I look back upon my own work,
and formulate the impression left upon my mind by
familiarity with the songs I have translated, the doubt
occurs whether some apology be not required for
having dragged these forth from antiquarian obscurity.

The truth is that there is very little that is elevated
in the lyrics of the Goliardi. They are almost wholly
destitute of domestic piety, of patriotism, of virtuous
impulse, of heroic resolve. The greatness of an epoch

which throbbed with the enthusiasms of the Crusades, which gave birth to a Francis and a Dominic, which witnessed the manly resistance offered by the Lombard burghs to the Teutonic Emperor, the formation of Northern France into a solid monarchy, and the victorious struggle of the Papacy against the Empire, finds but rare expression in this poetry. From the *Carmina Burana* we cull one chant indeed on Saladin, one spirited lament for Richard Cœur de Lion; but their general tone is egotistic.

Even the satires, so remarkable for boldness, are directed against those ecclesiastical abuses which touched the interests of the clerkly classes—against simony, avarice, venality in the Roman Curia, against the ambition of prelates and the effort to make princely benefices hereditary, rather than against the real sins of the Church—her wilful solidification of popular superstitions for the purposes of self-aggrandisement, her cruel persecution of free thought, and her deflection from the spirit of her Founder.

With regard to women, abundant examples have been adduced to illustrate the sensual and unromantic spirit of these lettered lovers. A note of undisguised materialism sounds throughout the large majority of their erotic songs. Tenderness of feeling is rarely present. The passion is one-sided, recognised as ephemeral, without a vista on the sanctities of life in common with the beloved object. Notable exceptions to the general rule are the lyrics I have printed above on pp. 74-77. But it would have been easier to confirm the impression of licentiousness than to multiply specimens of delicate sentiment, had I chosen to ransack the whole stores of the *Carmina Burana.*

It is not necessary to censure their lack of so-called chivalrous woman-worship. That artificial mood of emotion, though glorified by the literary art of greatest poets, has something pitiably unreal, incurably morbid, in its mysticism. But, putting this aside, we are still bound to notice the absence of that far more human self-devotion of man to woman which forms a conspicuous element in the Arthurian romances. The love of Tristram for Iseult, of Lancelot for Guinevere, of Beaumains for his lady, is alien to the Goliardic conception of intersexual relations. Nowhere do we find a trace of Arthur's vow imposed upon his knights : "never to do outrage, . . . and alway to do ladies, damosels, and gentlewomen succour upon pain of death." This manly respect for women, which was, if not precisely the purest, yet certainly the most fruitful social impulse of the Middle Ages, receives no expression in the *Carmina Vagorum.*

The reason is not far to seek. The Clerici were a class debarred from domesticity, devoted in theory to celibacy, in practice incapable of marriage. They were not so much unsocial or anti-social as extra-social ; and while they gave a loose rein to their appetites, they respected none of those ties, anticipated none of those home pleasures, which consecrate the animal desires in everyday existence as we know it. One of their most popular poems is a brutal monastic diatribe on matrimony, fouler in its stupid abuse of women, more unmanly in its sordid imputations, than any satire which emanated from

the corruption of Imperial Rome.[1] The cynicism of this
exhortation against marriage forms a proper supplement
to the other kind of cynicism which emerges in the
lyrics of triumphant seducers and light lovers.

But why then have I taken the trouble to translate
these songs, and to present them in such profusion to a
modern audience ?   It is because, after making all allowances for their want of great or noble feeling, due to the
peculiar medium from which they sprang, they are in
many ways realistically beautiful and in a strict sense
true to vulgar human nature.   They are the spontaneous
expression of careless, wanton, unreflective youth.   And
all this they were, too, in an age which we are apt to
regard as incapable of these very qualities.

The defects I have been at pains to indicate render
the Goliardic poems remarkable as documents for the
right understanding of the brilliant Renaissance epoch
which was destined to close the Middle Ages.   To the
best of them we may with certainty assign the seventy-
five years between 1150 and 1225.   In that period, so
fruitful of great efforts and of great results in the fields
of politics and thought and literature, efforts and results
foredoomed to partial frustration and to perverse mis-
application—in that potent space of time, so varied in
its intellectual and social manifestations, so pregnant
with good and evil, so rapid in mutations, so inde-
terminate between advance and retrogression—this
Goliardic poetry stands alone.   It occupies a position
of unique and isolated, if limited, interest ; because it
was no outcome of feudalism or ecclesiasticism ; because

[1] *Golias de Conjuge non ducenda*, Wright's *Mapes*, p. 77.

it has no tincture of chivalrous or mystic piety ; because
it implies no metaphysical determination ; because it is
pagan in the sense of being natural ; because it is
devoid of allegory, and, finally, because it is emphatically
humanistic.

In these respects it detaches itself from the artistic
and literary phenomena of the century which gave it
birth.   In these respects it anticipates the real eventual
Renaissance.

There are, indeed, points of contact between the Students' Songs and other products of the Middle Ages.
Scholastic quibblings upon words ; reiterated commonplaces about spring ; the brutal contempt for villeins ;
the frequent employment of hymn-rhythms and preoccupation with liturgical phrases—these show that the
Wandering Scholars were creatures of their age.   But
the qualities which this lyrical literature shares with that
of the court, the temple, or the schools are mainly
superficial ; whereas the vital inspiration, the specific
flavour, which render it noteworthy, are distinct and
self-evolved.   It is a premature, an unconscious effort
made by a limited class to achieve *per saltum* what was
slowly and laboriously wrought out by whole nations in
the fifteenth and sixteenth centuries.   Too precocious,
too complete within too narrow limits, it was doomed
to sterility.   Not the least singular fact about it is
that though the *Carmina Vagorum* continued to be
appreciated, they were neither imitated nor developed to
any definite extent after the period which I have
indicated.   They fell still-born upon the unreceptive
soil of European culture at that epoch.   Yet they fore-

shadowed the mental and moral attitude which Europe
was destined to assume when Italy through humanism
gave its tone to the Renaissance.

The Renaissance, in Italy as elsewhere, had far more
serious aims and enthusiasms in the direction of science,
refined self-culture, discoveries, analysis of man and
nature, than have always been ascribed to it.   The men
of that epoch did more hard work for the world,
conferred more sterling benefits on their posterity, than
those who study it chiefly from the point of view of
art are ready to admit.   But the mental atmosphere
in which those heroes lived and wrought was one of
carelessness with regard to moral duties and religious
aspirations, of exuberant delight in pleasure as an object
of existence.   The glorification of the body and the
senses, the repudiation of an ascetic tyranny which had
long in theory imposed impossible abstentions on the
carnal man, was a marked feature in their conception of
the world ; and connected with this was a return in no
merely superficial spirit to the antique paganism of
Greece and Rome.

These characteristics of the Renaissance we find
already outlined with surprising definiteness, and at the
same time with an almost childlike naïveté, a careless,
mirth-provoking nonchalance, in the *Carmina Vagorum*.
They remind us of the Italian lyrics which Lorenzo de'
Medici and Poliziano wrote for the Florentine populace ;
and though in form and artistic intention they differ
from the Latin verse of that period, their view of life
is not dissimilar to that of a Pontano or a Beccadelli.

Some folk may regard the things I have presented to

their view as ugly or insignificant, because they lack the
higher qualities of sentiment; others may over-value
them for precisely the same reason.   They seem to me
noteworthy as the first unmistakable sign of a change in
modern Europe which was inevitable and predestined,
as the first literary effort to restore the moral attitude
of antiquity which had been displaced by medieval
Christianity.   I also feel the special relation which
they bear to English poetry of the Elizabethan age—
a relation that has facilitated their conversion into
our language.

That Wandering Students of the twelfth century
should have transcended the limitations of their age;
that they should have absorbed so many elements of
life into their scheme of natural enjoyment as the artists
and scholars of the fifteenth; that they should have
theorised their appetites and impulses with Valla, have
produced masterpieces of poetry to rival Ariosto's, or
criticisms of society in the style of Rabelais, was not
to be expected.   What their lyrics prove by anticipation is the sincerity of the so-called paganism of the
Renaissance.   When we read them, we perceive that
that quality was substantially independent of the classical
revival; though the influences of antique literature were
eagerly seized upon as useful means for strengthening
and giving tone to an already potent revolt of nature
against hypocritical and palsy-stricken forms of spiritual
despotism.

APPENDIX

NOTE ON THE "ORDO VAGORUM" AND THE "ARCHIPOETA."

See Section vii. pp. 16–22, above.

IT seems desirable that I should enlarge upon some
topics which I treated somewhat summarily in Section
vii. I assumed that the Wandering Scholars regarded
themselves as a kind of Guild or Order; and for this
assumption the Songs Nos. 1, 2, 3, translated in Section
xiii. are a sufficient warrant. Yet the case might be
considerably strengthened. In the *Sequentia falsi evangelii secundum marcam argenti*[1] we read of the *Gens
Lusorum* or Tribe of Gamesters, which corresponds to
the *Secta Decii*,[2] the *Ordo Vagorum*, and the *Familia
Goliae*. Again, in Wright's *Walter Mapes*[3] there is
an epistle written from England by one Richardus
Goliardus to *Omnibus in Gallia Goliae discipulis*, introduc-
ing a friend, asking for information *ordo vester qualis
est*, and giving for the reason of this request *ne magis in
ordine indiscrete vivam*. He addresses his French
comrades as *pueri Goliae*, and winds up with good wishes
for the *socios sanctae confratriae*. Proofs might be
multiplied that the Wandering Students in Germany
also regarded themselves as a confraternity, with special

---

[1] Grimm's *Gedichte des Mittelalters*, p. 232.
[2] *Carm. Bur.*, p. 254.   [3] Page 69.

172

rules and ordinances. Of this, the curious parody of an episcopal letter, issued in 1209 by *Surianus, Praesul et Archiprimas,* to the *vagi clerici* of Austria, Styria, Bavaria, and Moravia is a notable example.[1]

I have treated Golias as the eponymous hero of this tribe, the chief of this confraternity. But it ought to be said that the name Golias occurs principally in English MSS., where the Goliardic poems are ascribed to *Golias Episcopus.* Elsewhere the same personage is spoken of as *Primas,* which is a title of dignity applying to a prelate with jurisdiction superior even to that of an archbishop. Grimm [2] quotes this phrase from a German chronicle : *Primas vagus multos versus edidit magistrales.* In the *Sequentia falsi evangelii* [3] we find twice repeated *Primas autem qui dicitur vilissimus.* The Venetian codex from which Grimm drew some of his texts [4] attributes the *Dispute of Thetis and Lyaeus* and the *Advice against Matrimony,* both of which passed in England under the name of Golias and afterwards of Walter Map, to *Primas Presbyter.*

With regard to this Primas, it is important to mention that Fra Salimbene in his Chronicle [5] gives a succinct account of him under the date 1233. It runs as follows : *Fuit his temporibus Primas canonicus coloniensis, magnus trutannus et magnus trufator, et maximus versificator et velox, qui, si dedisset cor suum ad diligendum Deum, magnus in litteratura divina fuisset, et utilis valde*

---

[1] Giesebrecht in *Allg. Monatschrift,* Jan. 1853, p. 35.
[2] Op. cit., p. 182.   [3] Ibid., p. 232.
[4] Ibid., pp. 238, 239.
  Published at Parma, 1857.

Ecclesiae Dei. Cujus Apocalypsim, quam fecerat, vidi, et alia scripta plura. After this passage follow some anecdotes, with quotations of verses extemporised by Primas, and lastly the whole of the Confession, translated by me at p. 53 above. Thus Salimbene, who was almost a contemporary author, attributes to Primas two of the most important poems which passed in England under the name of Golias, while the Venetian MS. ascribes two others of the same class to Primas Presbyter. It is also very noteworthy that Salimbene expressly calls this Primas a Canon of Cologne.

That this poet, whoever he was, had attained to celebrity in Italy (as well as in Germany) under the title of Primas, appears also from the following passage of a treatise by Thomas of Capua[1] on the Art of Writing : *Dictaminum vero tria sunt genera auctoribus diffinita, prosaicum scilicet, metricum et rithmicum ; prosaicum ut Cassiodori, metricum ut Virgilii, rithmicum ut Primatis.* Boccaccio was in all probability referring to the same Primas in the tale he told about *Primasso*,[2] who is described as a man of European reputation, and a great and rapid versifier. It is curious that just as Giraldus seems to have accepted *Golias* as the real name of this poet,[3] so Fra Salimbene, Thomas of Capua, and Boccaccio appear to use *Primas* as a Christian name.

The matter becomes still more complicated when we find, as we do, some of the same poems attributed in France to Walter of Lille, in England to Walter Map,

---

[1] See Novati, *Carmina Medii Aevi*, p. 8, note.
[2] *Decameron*, i. 7.   [3] See above, p. 21.

and further current under yet another title of dignity, that of *Archipoeta*.[1]

We can hardly avoid the conclusion that by Golias Episcopus, Primas, and Archipoeta one and the same person, occupying a prominent post in the Order, was denoted. He was the head of the Goliardic family, the Primate of the Wandering Students' Order, the Archpoet of these lettered minstrels. The rare excellence of the compositions ascribed to him caused them to be spread abroad, multiplied, and imitated in such fashion that it is now impossible to feel any certainty about the personality which underlay these titles.

Though we seem frequently upon the point of touching the real man, he constantly eludes our grasp. Who he was, whether he was one or many, remains a mystery. Whether the poems which bear one or other of his changing titles were really the work of a single writer, is also a matter for fruitless conjecture. We may take it for granted that he was not Walter Map; for Map was not a Canon of Cologne, not a follower of Reinald von Dassel, not a mark for the severe scorn of Giraldus. Similar reasoning renders it more than improbable that the Golias of Giraldus, the Primas of Salimbene, and the petitioner to Reinald should have been Walter of Lille.[2]

At the same time it is singular that the name of Walter should twice occur in Goliardic poems of a good

[1] Grimm, *op. cit.*, p. 189 *et seq.*
[2] Giesebrecht identifies Walter of Lille with the Archipoeta. But he seems to be unacquainted with Salimbene's Chronicle, and I agree with Hubatsch that he has not made out his point.

period.   One of these is the famous and beautiful
lament :—

> " Versa est in luctum—cithara Waltheri."

This exists in the MS. of the *Carmina Burana,* but not
in the Paris MS. of Walter's poems edited by Müldner.
It contains allusions to the poet's ejection from his place
in the Church—a misfortune which actually befell
Walter of Lille.   Grimm has printed another poem,
Saepe de miseria, in which the name of Walter occurs.[1]
It is introduced thus :

> " Hoc Gualtherus sub-prior
> Jubet in decretis."

Are we to infer from the designation *Sub-prior* that the
Walter of this poem held a post in the Order inferior
to that of the Primas ?

It is of importance in this connection to bear in mind
that five of the poems attributed in English MSS. to
Golias and Walter Map, namely, *Missus sum in vineam,*
Multiformis hominum, Fallax est et mobilis, A tauro tor-
rida, Heliconis rivulo, Tanto viro locuturi, among which
is the famous Apocalypse ascribed by Salimbene to
Primas, are given to Walter of Lille in the Paris MS.
edited by Müldner.[2]   They are distinguished by a
marked unity of style ; and what is also significant, a
lyric in this Paris MS., *Dum Gualterus aegrotaret,* introduces the poet's name in the same way as the *Versa est*
in luctum of the *Carmina Burana.*   Therefore, without
identifying Walter of Lille with the Primas, Archipoeta,

---

[1] Op. cit., p. 235, also in *Carm. Bur.,* p. 74.
[2] Hannover, 1859.

and Golias, we must allow that his place in Goliardic literature is very considerable. But I am inclined to think that the weight of evidence favours chiefly the ascription of serious and satiric pieces to his pen. It is probable that the Archipoeta, the follower of Reinald von Dassel, the man who composed the most vigorous Goliardic poem we possess, and gave the impulse of his genius to that style of writing, was not the Walter of the *Versa est in luctum* or of *Dum Gualterus aegrotaret.* That Walter must have been somewhat his junior ; and it is not unreasonable to assume that he was Walter of Lille, who may perhaps be further identified with the *Gualtherus sub-prior* of the poem on the author's poverty. This Walter's Latin designation, *Gualtherus de Insula,* helps, as I have observed above,[1] to explain the attribution of the Goliardic poems in general to Walter Map by English scribes of the fifteenth century.

After all, it is safer to indulge in no constructive speculations where the matter of inquiry is both vague and meagre. One thing appears tolerably manifest ; that many hands of very various dexterity contributed to form the whole body of songs which we call Goliardic. It is also clear that the Clerici Vagi considered themselves a confraternity, and that they burlesqued the institutions of a religious order, pretending to honour and obey a primate or bishop, to whom the nickname of Golias was given at the period in which they flourished most. Viewed in his literary capacity, this chief was further designated as the Archpoet. Of his personality we know as little as we do of that of Homer.

[1] Page 22.

BOOKS ON GOLIARDIC LITERATURE

Carmina Burana. Stuttgart. 1847.

Thomas Wright. The Latin Poems commonly attributed to Walter Mapes. Camden Society. 1841.

—— Anecdota Literaria. London. 1844.

—— Early Mysteries, etc. London. 1844.

Edélstand du Méril. Poésies Populaires Latines Antérieures au Douzième Siècle. Paris. 1843.

—— Poésies Populaires Latines du Moyen Age. Paris. 1847.   ——

—— Poésies Inédites du Moyen Age. Paris. 1854.

Jacob Grimm. Gedichte des Mittelalters auf König Friedrich I., den Staufer. Berlin. 1843.

H. Hagen. Carmina Medii Aevi Max. Part. Inedita. Bern. 1877.

F. Novati. Carmina Medii Aevi. Firenze. 1883.

Mone. Anzeiger, vii.

W. Müldener. Die Zehn Gedichte von Walther von Lille. Hannover. 1859.

Champollion-Figeac. Hilarii Versus et Ludi. Paris. 1838.

Gaudeamus. Leipzig. 1879.

Carmina Clericorum. Heilbronn. 1880.

A. P. Von Bärnstein. Carmina Burana Selecta. 1880.

—— Ubi sunt qui ante nos? Würtzburg. 1881.

Giesebrecht. Die Vaganten. Allg. Monatscrift für W. und K. 1853.

O. Hubatsch. Die Lateinischen Vagantenlieder. Görlitz. 1870.

A. Bartoli. I Precursori del Rinascimento. Firenze. 1876.

Allgemeines Deutsches Commersbuch.

TABLE OF SONGS TRANSLATED IN THIS VOLUME

N.B.—In order to facilitate the comparison between my translations and the originals, I have made the following table. The first column gives the number of the song and the second the page in this book ; the third column gives the beginning of each song in English ; the fourth gives the beginning of each song in Latin. The references in the fifth column are to the little anthology called *Gaudeamus* (Leipzig, Teubner, 1879); those in the sixth column are to the printed edition of the Benedictbeuern Codex, which goes by the title of *Carmina Burana* (Stuttgart, auf Kosten des Literarischen Vereins, Hering & Co. printers, 1847).

No.	Page	English.	Latin.	Gaud.	Car. Bur.
				Page	Page
1	40	At the mandate . .	Cum in orbem .	3	251
2	45	Once, it was . .	Olim nostrum .	6	...
3	48	I, a wandering . .	Exul ego .	178	50
4	50	We in our . .	Nos vagabunduli .	195	...
5	53	Boiling in my . .	Aestuans .	34	67
6	63	Spring is coming .	Ver redit . .	88	178
7	64	These hours of . .	Tempus est . .	100	211
8	66	Take your pleasure .	Congaudentes .	90	166
9	66	Winter's untruth .	Vetus error .	86	...
10	67	Winter, now . .	Cedit hiems .	85	177
11	68	Now the fields . .	Jamjam virent .	89	184
12	69	Spring returns . .	Ecce gratum .	84	183
13	70	Vernal hours . .	Vernum tempus .	81	...
14	71	Hail thou . . .	Salve ver . .	...	193
15	73	Summer sweet . .	Dum aestas .	97	196
16	74	The blithe young year	Anni novi .	...	145
17	75	Now the sun . .	Omnia sol .	109	177
18	76	In the spring . .	Veris dulcis .	...	195
19	77	With so sweet . .	De pollicito .	103	206
20	78	Wide the lime-tree .	Late pandit .	...	185
21	81	Yonder choir of .	Ecce chorus .	...	118
22	82	Meadows bloom .	Virent prata .	98	189
23	84	Cast aside . . .	Omittamus studia .	82	137
24	87	There went out . .	Exiit diluculo .	120	155
25	87	In the summer's .	Aestivali sub .	125	145
26	89	All the woods . .	Florent omnes .	93	182
27	93	When the lamp . .	Dum Dianae .	...	124
28	96	In the spring-time .	Anni parte .	...	155
29	100	On their steeds . .	Equitabant .	...	162
30	106	Take thou . . .	Suscipe Flos .	...	217
31	107	Come to me . .	Veni veni .	102	208
32	109	Lydia bright . .	Lydia bella .	96	...

TABLE OF SONGS—*continued*

* The original of this song will be found in Geiger, *Humanismus und Renaissance*, p. 414.
† The original will be found in Moll, *Hymnarium*, p. 138.

A CATALOG OF SELECTED DOVER
BOOKS IN ALL FIELDS OF INTEREST

CONCERNING THE SPIRITUAL IN ART, Wassily Kandinsky. Pioneering work by father of abstract art. Thoughts on color theory, nature of art. Analysis of earlier masters. 12 illustrations. 80pp. of text. 5⅜ x 8½. 23411-8

ANIMALS: 1,419 Copyright-Free Illustrations of Mammals, Birds, Fish, Insects, etc., Jim Harter (ed.). Clear wood engravings present, in extremely lifelike poses, over 1,000 species of animals. One of the most extensive pictorial sourcebooks of its kind. Captions. Index. 284pp. 9 x 12. 23766-4

CELTIC ART: The Methods of Construction, George Bain. Simple geometric techniques for making Celtic interlacements, spirals, Kells-type initials, animals, humans, etc. Over 500 illustrations. 160pp. 9 x 12. (Available in U.S. only.) 22923-8

AN ATLAS OF ANATOMY FOR ARTISTS, Fritz Schider. Most thorough reference work on art anatomy in the world. Hundreds of illustrations, including selections from works by Vesalius, Leonardo, Goya, Ingres, Michelangelo, others. 593 illustrations. 192pp. 7⅛ x 10¼. 20241-0

CELTIC HAND STROKE-BY-STROKE (Irish Half-Uncial from "The Book of Kells"): An Arthur Baker Calligraphy Manual, Arthur Baker. Complete guide to creating each letter of the alphabet in distinctive Celtic manner. Covers hand position, strokes, pens, inks, paper, more. Illustrated. 48pp. 8¼ x 11. 24336-2

EASY ORIGAMI, John Montroll. Charming collection of 32 projects (hat, cup, pelican, piano, swan, many more) specially designed for the novice origami hobbyist. Clearly illustrated easy-to-follow instructions insure that even beginning papercrafters will achieve successful results. 48pp. 8¼ x 11. 27298-2

THE COMPLETE BOOK OF BIRDHOUSE CONSTRUCTION FOR WOODWORKERS, Scott D. Campbell. Detailed instructions, illustrations, tables. Also data on bird habitat and instinct patterns. Bibliography. 3 tables. 63 illustrations in 15 figures. 48pp. 5¼ x 8½. 24407-5

BLOOMINGDALE'S ILLUSTRATED 1886 CATALOG: Fashions, Dry Goods and Housewares, Bloomingdale Brothers. Famed merchants' extremely rare catalog depicting about 1,700 products: clothing, housewares, firearms, dry goods, jewelry, more. Invaluable for dating, identifying vintage items. Also, copyright-free graphics for artists, designers. Co-published with Henry Ford Museum & Greenfield Village. 160pp. 8¼ x 11. 25780-0

HISTORIC COSTUME IN PICTURES, Braun & Schneider. Over 1,450 costumed figures in clearly detailed engravings–from dawn of civilization to end of 19th century. Captions. Many folk costumes. 256pp. 8⅜ x 11¾. 23150-X

CATALOG OF DOVER BOOKS

STICKLEY CRAFTSMAN FURNITURE CATALOGS, Gustav Stickley and L. & J. G. Stickley. Beautiful, functional furniture in two authentic catalogs from 1910. 594 illustrations, including 277 photos, show settles, rockers, armchairs, reclining chairs, bookcases, desks, tables. 183pp. 6½ x 9¼.   23838-5

AMERICAN LOCOMOTIVES IN HISTORIC PHOTOGRAPHS: 1858 to 1949, Ron Ziel (ed.). A rare collection of 126 meticulously detailed official photographs, called "builder portraits," of American locomotives that majestically chronicle the rise of steam locomotive power in America. Introduction. Detailed captions. xi+ 129pp. 9 x 12.   27393-8

AMERICA'S LIGHTHOUSES: An Illustrated History, Francis Ross Holland, Jr. Delightfully written, profusely illustrated fact-filled survey of over 200 American light-houses since 1716. History, anecdotes, technological advances, more. 240pp. 8 x 10¾.
25576-X

TOWARDS A NEW ARCHITECTURE, Le Corbusier. Pioneering manifesto by founder of "International School." Technical and aesthetic theories, views of industry, economics, relation of form to function, "mass-production split" and much more. Profusely illustrated. 320pp. 6⅛ x 9¼. (Available in U.S. only.)   25023-7

HOW THE OTHER HALF LIVES, Jacob Riis. Famous journalistic record, exposing poverty and degradation of New York slums around 1900, by major social reformer. 100 striking and influential photographs. 233pp. 10 x 7⅞.   22012-5

FRUIT KEY AND TWIG KEY TO TREES AND SHRUBS, William M. Harlow. One of the handiest and most widely used identification aids. Fruit key covers 120 deciduous and evergreen species; twig key 160 deciduous species. Easily used. Over 300 photographs. 126pp. 5⅜ x 8½.   20511-8

COMMON BIRD SONGS, Dr. Donald J. Borror. Songs of 60 most common U.S. birds: robins, sparrows, cardinals, bluejays, finches, more—arranged in order of increasing complexity. Up to 9 variations of songs of each species.
Cassette and manual 99911-4

ORCHIDS AS HOUSE PLANTS, Rebecca Tyson Northen. Grow cattleyas and many other kinds of orchids—in a window, in a case, or under artificial light. 63 illustrations. 148pp. 5⅜ x 8½.   23261-1

MONSTER MAZES, Dave Phillips. Masterful mazes at four levels of difficulty. Avoid deadly perils and evil creatures to find magical treasures. Solutions for all 32 exciting illustrated puzzles. 48pp. 8¼ x 11.   26005-4

MOZART'S DON GIOVANNI (DOVER OPERA LIBRETTO SERIES), Wolfgang Amadeus Mozart. Introduced and translated by Ellen H. Bleiler. Standard Italian libretto, with complete English translation. Convenient and thoroughly portable—an ideal companion for reading along with a recording or the performance itself. Introduction. List of characters. Plot summary. 121pp. 5¼ x 8½.   24944-1

TECHNICAL MANUAL AND DICTIONARY OF CLASSICAL BALLET, Gail Grant. Defines, explains, comments on steps, movements, poses and concepts. 15-page pictorial section. Basic book for student, viewer. 127pp. 5⅜ x 8½.   21843-0

THE CLARINET AND CLARINET PLAYING, David Pino. Lively, comprehensive work features suggestions about technique, musicianship, and musical interpretation, as well as guidelines for teaching, making your own reeds, and preparing for public performance. Includes an intriguing look at clarinet history. "A godsend," *The Clarinet,* Journal of the International Clarinet Society. Appendixes. 7 illus. 320pp. 5⅜ x 8½. 40270-3

HOLLYWOOD GLAMOR PORTRAITS, John Kobal (ed.). 145 photos from 1926-49. Harlow, Gable, Bogart, Bacall; 94 stars in all. Full background on photographers, technical aspects. 160pp. 8⅜ x 11¼. 23352-9

THE ANNOTATED CASEY AT THE BAT: A Collection of Ballads about the Mighty Casey/Third, Revised Edition, Martin Gardner (ed.). Amusing sequels and parodies of one of America's best-loved poems: Casey's Revenge, Why Casey Whiffed, Casey's Sister at the Bat, others. 256pp. 5⅜ x 8½. 28598-7

THE RAVEN AND OTHER FAVORITE POEMS, Edgar Allan Poe. Over 40 of the author's most memorable poems: "The Bells," "Ulalume," "Israfel," "To Helen," "The Conqueror Worm," "Eldorado," "Annabel Lee," many more. Alphabetic lists of titles and first lines. 64pp. 5³⁄₁₆ x 8¼. 26685-0

PERSONAL MEMOIRS OF U. S. GRANT, Ulysses Simpson Grant. Intelligent, deeply moving firsthand account of Civil War campaigns, considered by many the finest military memoirs ever written. Includes letters, historic photographs, maps and more. 528pp. 6⅛ x 9¼. 28587-1

ANCIENT EGYPTIAN MATERIALS AND INDUSTRIES, A. Lucas and J. Harris. Fascinating, comprehensive, thoroughly documented text describes this ancient civilization's vast resources and the processes that incorporated them in daily life, including the use of animal products, building materials, cosmetics, perfumes and incense, fibers, glazed ware, glass and its manufacture, materials used in the mummification process, and much more. 544pp. 6⅛ x 9¼. (Available in U.S. only.) 40446-3

RUSSIAN STORIES/RUSSKIE RASSKAZY: A Dual-Language Book, edited by Gleb Struve. Twelve tales by such masters as Chekhov, Tolstoy, Dostoevsky, Pushkin, others. Excellent word-for-word English translations on facing pages, plus teaching and study aids, Russian/English vocabulary, biographical/critical introductions, more. 416pp. 5⅜ x 8½. 26244-8

PHILADELPHIA THEN AND NOW: 60 Sites Photographed in the Past and Present, Kenneth Finkel and Susan Oyama. Rare photographs of City Hall, Logan Square, Independence Hall, Betsy Ross House, other landmarks juxtaposed with contemporary views. Captures changing face of historic city. Introduction. Captions. 128pp. 8¼ x 11. 25790-8

AIA ARCHITECTURAL GUIDE TO NASSAU AND SUFFOLK COUNTIES, LONG ISLAND, The American Institute of Architects, Long Island Chapter, and the Society for the Preservation of Long Island Antiquities. Comprehensive, well-researched and generously illustrated volume brings to life over three centuries of Long Island's great architectural heritage. More than 240 photographs with authoritative, extensively detailed captions. 176pp. 8¼ x 11. 26946-9

NORTH AMERICAN INDIAN LIFE: Customs and Traditions of 23 Tribes, Elsie Clews Parsons (ed.). 27 fictionalized essays by noted anthropologists examine religion, customs, government, additional facets of life among the Winnebago, Crow, Zuni, Eskimo, other tribes. 480pp. 6⅛ x 9¼. 27377-6

FRANK LLOYD WRIGHT'S DANA HOUSE, Donald Hoffmann. Pictorial essay of residential masterpiece with over 160 interior and exterior photos, plans, elevations, sketches and studies. 128pp. 9¼ x 10¾. 29120-0

THE MALE AND FEMALE FIGURE IN MOTION: 60 Classic Photographic Sequences, Eadweard Muybridge. 60 true-action photographs of men and women walking, running, climbing, bending, turning, etc., reproduced from rare 19th-century masterpiece. vi + 121pp. 9 x 12. 24745-7

1001 QUESTIONS ANSWERED ABOUT THE SEASHORE, N. J. Berrill and Jacquelyn Berrill. Queries answered about dolphins, sea snails, sponges, starfish, fishes, shore birds, many others. Covers appearance, breeding, growth, feeding, much more. 305pp. 5¼ x 8¼. 23366-9

ATTRACTING BIRDS TO YOUR YARD, William J. Weber. Easy-to-follow guide offers advice on how to attract the greatest diversity of birds: birdhouses, feeders, water and waterers, much more. 96pp. 5³/₁₆ x 8¼. 28927-3

MEDICINAL AND OTHER USES OF NORTH AMERICAN PLANTS: A Historical Survey with Special Reference to the Eastern Indian Tribes, Charlotte Erichsen-Brown. Chronological historical citations document 500 years of usage of plants, trees, shrubs native to eastern Canada, northeastern U.S. Also complete identifying information. 343 illustrations. 544pp. 6½ x 9¼. 25951-X

STORYBOOK MAZES, Dave Phillips. 23 stories and mazes on two-page spreads: Wizard of Oz, Treasure Island, Robin Hood, etc. Solutions. 64pp. 8¼ x 11. 23628-5

AMERICAN NEGRO SONGS: 230 Folk Songs and Spirituals, Religious and Secular, John W. Work. This authoritative study traces the African influences of songs sung and played by black Americans at work, in church, and as entertainment. The author discusses the lyric significance of such songs as "Swing Low, Sweet Chariot," "John Henry," and others and offers the words and music for 230 songs. Bibliography. Index of Song Titles. 272pp. 6½ x 9¼. 40271-1

MOVIE-STAR PORTRAITS OF THE FORTIES, John Kobal (ed.). 163 glamor, studio photos of 106 stars of the 1940s: Rita Hayworth, Ava Gardner, Marlon Brando, Clark Gable, many more. 176pp. 8⅜ x 11¼. 23546-7

BENCHLEY LOST AND FOUND, Robert Benchley. Finest humor from early 30s, about pet peeves, child psychologists, post office and others. Mostly unavailable elsewhere. 73 illustrations by Peter Arno and others. 183pp. 5⅜ x 8½. 22410-4

YEKL and THE IMPORTED BRIDEGROOM AND OTHER STORIES OF YIDDISH NEW YORK, Abraham Cahan. Film Hester Street based on *Yekl* (1896). Novel, other stories among first about Jewish immigrants on N.Y.'s East Side. 240pp. 5⅜ x 8½. 22427-9

SELECTED POEMS, Walt Whitman. Generous sampling from *Leaves of Grass*. Twenty-four poems include "I Hear America Singing," "Song of the Open Road," "I Sing the Body Electric," "When Lilacs Last in the Dooryard Bloom'd," "O Captain! My Captain!"—all reprinted from an authoritative edition. Lists of titles and first lines. 128pp. 5³/₁₆ x 8¼. 26878-0

THE BEST TALES OF HOFFMANN, E. T. A. Hoffmann. 10 of Hoffmann's most important stories: "Nutcracker and the King of Mice," "The Golden Flowerpot," etc. 458pp. 5⅜ x 8½. 21793-0

FROM FETISH TO GOD IN ANCIENT EGYPT, E. A. Wallis Budge. Rich detailed survey of Egyptian conception of "God" and gods, magic, cult of animals, Osiris, more. Also, superb English translations of hymns and legends. 240 illustrations. 545pp. 5⅜ x 8½. 25803-3

FRENCH STORIES/CONTES FRANÇAIS: A Dual-Language Book, Wallace Fowlie. Ten stories by French masters, Voltaire to Camus: "Micromegas" by Voltaire; "The Atheist's Mass" by Balzac; "Minuet" by de Maupassant; "The Guest" by Camus, six more. Excellent English translations on facing pages. Also French-English vocabulary list, exercises, more. 352pp. 5⅜ x 8½. 26443-2

CHICAGO AT THE TURN OF THE CENTURY IN PHOTOGRAPHS: 122 Historic Views from the Collections of the Chicago Historical Society, Larry A. Viskochil. Rare large-format prints offer detailed views of City Hall, State Street, the Loop, Hull House, Union Station, many other landmarks, circa 1904-1913. Introduction. Captions. Maps. 144pp. 9⅜ x 12¼. 24656-6

OLD BROOKLYN IN EARLY PHOTOGRAPHS, 1865-1929, William Lee Younger. Luna Park, Gravesend race track, construction of Grand Army Plaza, moving of Hotel Brighton, etc. 157 previously unpublished photographs. 165pp. 8⅞ x 11¾. 23587-4

THE MYTHS OF THE NORTH AMERICAN INDIANS, Lewis Spence. Rich anthology of the myths and legends of the Algonquins, Iroquois, Pawnees and Sioux, prefaced by an extensive historical and ethnological commentary. 36 illustrations. 480pp. 5⅜ x 8½. 25967-6

AN ENCYCLOPEDIA OF BATTLES: Accounts of Over 1,560 Battles from 1479 B.C. to the Present, David Eggenberger. Essential details of every major battle in recorded history from the first battle of Megiddo in 1479 B.C. to Grenada in 1984. List of Battle Maps. New Appendix covering the years 1967-1984. Index. 99 illustrations. 544pp. 6½ x 9¼. 24913-1

SAILING ALONE AROUND THE WORLD, Captain Joshua Slocum. First man to sail around the world, alone, in small boat. One of great feats of seamanship told in delightful manner. 67 illustrations. 294pp. 5⅜ x 8½. 20326-3

ANARCHISM AND OTHER ESSAYS, Emma Goldman. Powerful, penetrating, prophetic essays on direct action, role of minorities, prison reform, puritan hypocrisy, violence, etc. 271pp. 5⅜ x 8½. 22484-8

MYTHS OF THE HINDUS AND BUDDHISTS, Ananda K. Coomaraswamy and Sister Nivedita. Great stories of the epics; deeds of Krishna, Shiva, taken from puranas, Vedas, folk tales; etc. 32 illustrations. 400pp. 5⅜ x 8½. 21759-0

THE TRAUMA OF BIRTH, Otto Rank. Rank's controversial thesis that anxiety neurosis is caused by profound psychological trauma which occurs at birth. 256pp. 5⅜ x 8½. 27974-X

A THEOLOGICO-POLITICAL TREATISE, Benedict Spinoza. Also contains unfinished Political Treatise. Great classic on religious liberty, theory of government on common consent. R. Elwes translation. Total of 421pp. 5⅜ x 8½. 20249-6

MY BONDAGE AND MY FREEDOM, Frederick Douglass. Born a slave, Douglass became outspoken force in antislavery movement. The best of Douglass' autobiographies. Graphic description of slave life. 464pp. 5⅜ x 8½. 22457-0

FOLLOWING THE EQUATOR: A Journey Around the World, Mark Twain. Fascinating humorous account of 1897 voyage to Hawaii, Australia, India, New Zealand, etc. Ironic, bemused reports on peoples, customs, climate, flora and fauna, politics, much more. 197 illustrations. 720pp. 5⅜ x 8½. 26113-1

THE PEOPLE CALLED SHAKERS, Edward D. Andrews. Definitive study of Shakers: origins, beliefs, practices, dances, social organization, furniture and crafts, etc. 33 illustrations. 351pp. 5⅜ x 8½. 21081-2

THE MYTHS OF GREECE AND ROME, H. A. Guerber. A classic of mythology, generously illustrated, long prized for its simple, graphic, accurate retelling of the principal myths of Greece and Rome, and for its commentary on their origins and significance. With 64 illustrations by Michelangelo, Raphael, Titian, Rubens, Canova, Bernini and others. 480pp. 5⅜ x 8½. 27584-1

PSYCHOLOGY OF MUSIC, Carl E. Seashore. Classic work discusses music as a medium from psychological viewpoint. Clear treatment of physical acoustics, auditory apparatus, sound perception, development of musical skills, nature of musical feeling, host of other topics. 88 figures. 408pp. 5⅜ x 8½. 21851-1

THE PHILOSOPHY OF HISTORY, Georg W. Hegel. Great classic of Western thought develops concept that history is not chance but rational process, the evolution of freedom. 457pp. 5⅜ x 8½. 20112-0

THE BOOK OF TEA, Kakuzo Okakura. Minor classic of the Orient: entertaining, charming explanation, interpretation of traditional Japanese culture in terms of tea ceremony. 94pp. 5⅜ x 8½. 20070-1

LIFE IN ANCIENT EGYPT, Adolf Erman. Fullest, most thorough, detailed older account with much not in more recent books, domestic life, religion, magic, medicine, commerce, much more. Many illustrations reproduce tomb paintings, carvings, hieroglyphs, etc. 597pp. 5⅜ x 8½. 22632-8

SUNDIALS, Their Theory and Construction, Albert Waugh. Far and away the best, most thorough coverage of ideas, mathematics concerned, types, construction, adjusting anywhere. Simple, nontechnical treatment allows even children to build several of these dials. Over 100 illustrations. 230pp. 5⅜ x 8½. 22947-5

THEORETICAL HYDRODYNAMICS, L. M. Milne-Thomson. Classic exposition of the mathematical theory of fluid motion, applicable to both hydrodynamics and aerodynamics. Over 600 exercises. 768pp. 6⅛ x 9¼. 68970-0

SONGS OF EXPERIENCE: Facsimile Reproduction with 26 Plates in Full Color, William Blake. 26 full-color plates from a rare 1826 edition. Includes "The Tyger," "London," "Holy Thursday," and other poems. Printed text of poems. 48pp. 5¼ x 7. 24636-1

OLD-TIME VIGNETTES IN FULL COLOR, Carol Belanger Grafton (ed.). Over 390 charming, often sentimental illustrations, selected from archives of Victorian graphics—pretty women posing, children playing, food, flowers, kittens and puppies, smiling cherubs, birds and butterflies, much more. All copyright-free. 48pp. 9¼ x 12¼. 27269-9

PERSPECTIVE FOR ARTISTS, Rex Vicat Cole. Depth, perspective of sky and sea, shadows, much more, not usually covered. 391 diagrams, 81 reproductions of drawings and paintings. 279pp. 5⅜ x 8½. 22487-2

DRAWING THE LIVING FIGURE, Joseph Sheppard. Innovative approach to artistic anatomy focuses on specifics of surface anatomy, rather than muscles and bones. Over 170 drawings of live models in front, back and side views, and in widely varying poses. Accompanying diagrams. 177 illustrations. Introduction. Index. 144pp. 8⅜ x11¼. 26723-7

GOTHIC AND OLD ENGLISH ALPHABETS: 100 Complete Fonts, Dan X. Solo. Add power, elegance to posters, signs, other graphics with 100 stunning copyright-free alphabets: Blackstone, Dolbey, Germania, 97 more–including many lower-case, numerals, punctuation marks. 104pp. 8⅛ x 11. 24695-7

HOW TO DO BEADWORK, Mary White. Fundamental book on craft from simple projects to five-bead chains and woven works. 106 illustrations. 142pp. 5⅜ x 8. 20697-1

THE BOOK OF WOOD CARVING, Charles Marshall Sayers. Finest book for beginners discusses fundamentals and offers 34 designs. "Absolutely first rate . . . well thought out and well executed."–E. J. Tangerman. 118pp. 7¾ x 10⅝. 23654-4

ILLUSTRATED CATALOG OF CIVIL WAR MILITARY GOODS: Union Army Weapons, Insignia, Uniform Accessories, and Other Equipment, Schuyler, Hartley, and Graham. Rare, profusely illustrated 1846 catalog includes Union Army uniform and dress regulations, arms and ammunition, coats, insignia, flags, swords, rifles, etc. 226 illustrations. 160pp. 9 x 12. 24939-5

WOMEN'S FASHIONS OF THE EARLY 1900s: An Unabridged Republication of "New York Fashions, 1909," National Cloak & Suit Co. Rare catalog of mail-order fashions documents women's and children's clothing styles shortly after the turn of the century. Captions offer full descriptions, prices. Invaluable resource for fashion, costume historians. Approximately 725 illustrations. 128pp. 8⅜ x 11¼. 27276-1

THE 1912 AND 1915 GUSTAV STICKLEY FURNITURE CATALOGS, Gustav Stickley. With over 200 detailed illustrations and descriptions, these two catalogs are essential reading and reference materials and identification guides for Stickley furniture. Captions cite materials, dimensions and prices. 112pp. 6½ x 9¼. 26676-1

EARLY AMERICAN LOCOMOTIVES, John H. White, Jr. Finest locomotive engravings from early 19th century: historical (1804–74), main-line (after 1870), special, foreign, etc. 147 plates. 142pp. 11⅜ x 8¼. 22772-3

THE TALL SHIPS OF TODAY IN PHOTOGRAPHS, Frank O. Braynard. Lavishly illustrated tribute to nearly 100 majestic contemporary sailing vessels: Amerigo Vespucci, Clearwater, Constitution, Eagle, Mayflower, Sea Cloud, Victory, many more. Authoritative captions provide statistics, background on each ship. 190 black-and-white photographs and illustrations. Introduction. 128pp. 8⅞ x 11¾. 27163-3

LITTLE BOOK OF EARLY AMERICAN CRAFTS AND TRADES, Peter Stockham (ed.). 1807 children's book explains crafts and trades: baker, hatter, cooper, potter, and many others. 23 copperplate illustrations. 140pp. 4⅝ x 6. 23336-7

VICTORIAN FASHIONS AND COSTUMES FROM HARPER'S BAZAR, 1867–1898, Stella Blum (ed.). Day costumes, evening wear, sports clothes, shoes, hats, other accessories in over 1,000 detailed engravings. 320pp. 9⅜ x 12¼. 22990-4

GUSTAV STICKLEY, THE CRAFTSMAN, Mary Ann Smith. Superb study surveys broad scope of Stickley's achievement, especially in architecture. Design philosophy, rise and fall of the Craftsman empire, descriptions and floor plans for many Craftsman houses, more. 86 black-and-white halftones. 31 line illustrations. Introduction 208pp. 6½ x 9¼. 27210-9

THE LONG ISLAND RAIL ROAD IN EARLY PHOTOGRAPHS, Ron Ziel. Over 220 rare photos, informative text document origin (1844) and development of rail service on Long Island. Vintage views of early trains, locomotives, stations, passengers, crews, much more. Captions. 8⅞ x 11¾. 26301-0

VOYAGE OF THE LIBERDADE, Joshua Slocum. Great 19th-century mariner's thrilling, first-hand account of the wreck of his ship off South America, the 35-foot boat he built from the wreckage, and its remarkable voyage home. 128pp. 5⅜ x 8½. 40022-0

TEN BOOKS ON ARCHITECTURE, Vitruvius. The most important book ever written on architecture. Early Roman aesthetics, technology, classical orders, site selection, all other aspects. Morgan translation. 331pp. 5⅜ x 8½. 20645-9

THE HUMAN FIGURE IN MOTION, Eadweard Muybridge. More than 4,500 stopped-action photos, in action series, showing undraped men, women, children jumping, lying down, throwing, sitting, wrestling, carrying, etc. 390pp. 7⅞ x 10⅝. 20204-6 Clothbd.

TREES OF THE EASTERN AND CENTRAL UNITED STATES AND CANADA, William M. Harlow. Best one-volume guide to 140 trees. Full descriptions, woodlore, range, etc. Over 600 illustrations. Handy size. 288pp. 4½ x 6⅜. 20395-6

SONGS OF WESTERN BIRDS, Dr. Donald J. Borror. Complete song and call repertoire of 60 western species, including flycatchers, juncoes, cactus wrens, many more–includes fully illustrated booklet. Cassette and manual 99913-0

GROWING AND USING HERBS AND SPICES, Milo Miloradovich. Versatile handbook provides all the information needed for cultivation and use of all the herbs and spices available in North America. 4 illustrations. Index. Glossary. 236pp. 5⅜ x 8½. 25058-X

BIG BOOK OF MAZES AND LABYRINTHS, Walter Shepherd. 50 mazes and labyrinths in all–classical, solid, ripple, and more–in one great volume. Perfect inexpensive puzzler for clever youngsters. Full solutions. 112pp. 8⅛ x 11. 22951-3

PIANO TUNING, J. Cree Fischer. Clearest, best book for beginner, amateur. Simple repairs, raising dropped notes, tuning by easy method of flattened fifths. No previous skills needed. 4 illustrations. 201pp. 5⅜ x 8½. 23267-0

HINTS TO SINGERS, Lillian Nordica. Selecting the right teacher, developing confidence, overcoming stage fright, and many other important skills receive thoughtful discussion in this indispensible guide, written by a world-famous diva of four decades' experience. 96pp. 5⅜ x 8½. 40094-8

THE COMPLETE NONSENSE OF EDWARD LEAR, Edward Lear. All nonsense limericks, zany alphabets, Owl and Pussycat, songs, nonsense botany, etc., illustrated by Lear. Total of 320pp. 5⅜ x 8½. (Available in U.S. only.) 20167-8

VICTORIAN PARLOUR POETRY: An Annotated Anthology, Michael R. Turner. 117 gems by Longfellow, Tennyson, Browning, many lesser-known poets. "The Village Blacksmith," "Curfew Must Not Ring Tonight," "Only a Baby Small," dozens more, often difficult to find elsewhere. Index of poets, titles, first lines. xxiii + 325pp. 5⅝ x 8¼. 27044-0

DUBLINERS, James Joyce. Fifteen stories offer vivid, tightly focused observations of the lives of Dublin's poorer classes. At least one, "The Dead," is considered a masterpiece. Reprinted complete and unabridged from standard edition. 160pp. 5$\frac{3}{16}$ x 8¼. 26870-5

GREAT WEIRD TALES: 14 Stories by Lovecraft, Blackwood, Machen and Others, S. T. Joshi (ed.). 14 spellbinding tales, including "The Sin Eater," by Fiona McLeod, "The Eye Above the Mantel," by Frank Belknap Long, as well as renowned works by R. H. Barlow, Lord Dunsany, Arthur Machen, W. C. Morrow and eight other masters of the genre. 256pp. 5⅜ x 8½. (Available in U.S. only.) 40436-6

THE BOOK OF THE SACRED MAGIC OF ABRAMELIN THE MAGE, translated by S. MacGregor Mathers. Medieval manuscript of ceremonial magic. Basic document in Aleister Crowley, Golden Dawn groups. 268pp. 5⅜ x 8½. 23211-5

NEW RUSSIAN-ENGLISH AND ENGLISH-RUSSIAN DICTIONARY, M. A. O'Brien. This is a remarkably handy Russian dictionary, containing a surprising amount of information, including over 70,000 entries. 366pp. 4½ x 6⅛. 20208-9

HISTORIC HOMES OF THE AMERICAN PRESIDENTS, Second, Revised Edition, Irvin Haas. A traveler's guide to American Presidential homes, most open to the public, depicting and describing homes occupied by every American President from George Washington to George Bush. With visiting hours, admission charges, travel routes. 175 photographs. Index. 160pp. 8¼ x 11. 26751-2

NEW YORK IN THE FORTIES, Andreas Feininger. 162 brilliant photographs by the well-known photographer, formerly with *Life* magazine. Commuters, shoppers, Times Square at night, much else from city at its peak. Captions by John von Hartz. 181pp. 9¼ x 10¾. 23585-8

INDIAN SIGN LANGUAGE, William Tomkins. Over 525 signs developed by Sioux and other tribes. Written instructions and diagrams. Also 290 pictographs. 111pp. 6⅛ x 9¼. 22029-X

ANATOMY: A Complete Guide for Artists, Joseph Sheppard. A master of figure drawing shows artists how to render human anatomy convincingly. Over 460 illustrations. 224pp. 8⅜ x 11¼. 27279-6

MEDIEVAL CALLIGRAPHY: Its History and Technique, Marc Drogin. Spirited history, comprehensive instruction manual covers 13 styles (ca. 4th century through 15th). Excellent photographs; directions for duplicating medieval techniques with modern tools. 224pp. 8⅜ x 11¼. 26142-5

DRIED FLOWERS: How to Prepare Them, Sarah Whitlock and Martha Rankin. Complete instructions on how to use silica gel, meal and borax, perlite aggregate, sand and borax, glycerine and water to create attractive permanent flower arrangements. 12 illustrations. 32pp. 5⅜ x 8½. 21802-3

EASY-TO-MAKE BIRD FEEDERS FOR WOODWORKERS, Scott D. Campbell. Detailed, simple-to-use guide for designing, constructing, caring for and using feeders. Text, illustrations for 12 classic and contemporary designs. 96pp. 5⅜ x 8½. 25847-5

SCOTTISH WONDER TALES FROM MYTH AND LEGEND, Donald A. Mackenzie. 16 lively tales tell of giants rumbling down mountainsides, of a magic wand that turns stone pillars into warriors, of gods and goddesses, evil hags, powerful forces and more. 240pp. 5⅜ x 8½. 29677-6

THE HISTORY OF UNDERCLOTHES, C. Willett Cunnington and Phyllis Cunnington. Fascinating, well-documented survey covering six centuries of English undergarments, enhanced with over 100 illustrations: 12th-century laced-up bodice, footed long drawers (1795), 19th-century bustles, 19th-century corsets for men, Victorian "bust improvers," much more. 272pp. 5⅜ x 8¼. 27124-2

ARTS AND CRAFTS FURNITURE: The Complete Brooks Catalog of 1912, Brooks Manufacturing Co. Photos and detailed descriptions of more than 150 now very collectible furniture designs from the Arts and Crafts movement depict davenports, settees, buffets, desks, tables, chairs, bedsteads, dressers and more, all built of solid, quarter-sawed oak. Invaluable for students and enthusiasts of antiques, Americana and the decorative arts. 80pp. 6½ x 9¼. 27471-3

WILBUR AND ORVILLE: A Biography of the Wright Brothers, Fred Howard. Definitive, crisply written study tells the full story of the brothers' lives and work. A vividly written biography, unparalleled in scope and color, that also captures the spirit of an extraordinary era. 560pp. 6⅛ x 9¼. 40297-5

THE ARTS OF THE SAILOR: Knotting, Splicing and Ropework, Hervey Garrett Smith. Indispensable shipboard reference covers tools, basic knots and useful hitches; handsewing and canvas work, more. Over 100 illustrations. Delightful reading for sea lovers. 256pp. 5⅜ x 8½. 26440-8

FRANK LLOYD WRIGHT'S FALLINGWATER: The House and Its History, Second, Revised Edition, Donald Hoffmann. A total revision–both in text and illustrations–of the standard document on Fallingwater, the boldest, most personal architectural statement of Wright's mature years, updated with valuable new material from the recently opened Frank Lloyd Wright Archives. "Fascinating"–*The New York Times*. 116 illustrations. 128pp. 9¼ x 10¾. 27430-6

CATALOG OF DOVER BOOKS

PHOTOGRAPHIC SKETCHBOOK OF THE CIVIL WAR, Alexander Gardner. 100 photos taken on field during the Civil War. Famous shots of Manassas Harper's Ferry, Lincoln, Richmond, slave pens, etc. 244pp. 10⅝ x 8¼. 22731-6

FIVE ACRES AND INDEPENDENCE, Maurice G. Kains. Great back-to-the-land classic explains basics of self-sufficient farming. The one book to get. 95 illustrations. 397pp. 5⅜ x 8½. 20974-1

SONGS OF EASTERN BIRDS, Dr. Donald J. Borror. Songs and calls of 60 species most common to eastern U.S.: warblers, woodpeckers, flycatchers, thrushes, larks, many more in high-quality recording. Cassette and manual 99912-2

A MODERN HERBAL, Margaret Grieve. Much the fullest, most exact, most useful compilation of herbal material. Gigantic alphabetical encyclopedia, from aconite to zedoary, gives botanical information, medical properties, folklore, economic uses, much else. Indispensable to serious reader. 161 illustrations. 888pp. 6½ x 9¼. 2-vol. set. (Available in U.S. only.) Vol. I: 22798-7
Vol. II: 22799-5

HIDDEN TREASURE MAZE BOOK, Dave Phillips. Solve 34 challenging mazes accompanied by heroic tales of adventure. Evil dragons, people-eating plants, blood-thirsty giants, many more dangerous adversaries lurk at every twist and turn. 34 mazes, stories, solutions. 48pp. 8¼ x 11. 24566-7

LETTERS OF W. A. MOZART, Wolfgang A. Mozart. Remarkable letters show bawdy wit, humor, imagination, musical insights, contemporary musical world; includes some letters from Leopold Mozart. 276pp. 5⅜ x 8½. 22859-2

BASIC PRINCIPLES OF CLASSICAL BALLET, Agrippina Vaganova. Great Russian theoretician, teacher explains methods for teaching classical ballet. 118 illustrations. 175pp. 5⅜ x 8½. 22036-2

THE JUMPING FROG, Mark Twain. Revenge edition. The original story of The Celebrated Jumping Frog of Calaveras County, a hapless French translation, and Twain's hilarious "retranslation" from the French. 12 illustrations. 66pp. 5⅜ x 8½. 22686-7

BEST REMEMBERED POEMS, Martin Gardner (ed.). The 126 poems in this superb collection of 19th- and 20th-century British and American verse range from Shelley's "To a Skylark" to the impassioned "Renascence" of Edna St. Vincent Millay and to Edward Lear's whimsical "The Owl and the Pussycat." 224pp. 5⅜ x 8½. 27165-X

COMPLETE SONNETS, William Shakespeare. Over 150 exquisite poems deal with love, friendship, the tyranny of time, beauty's evanescence, death and other themes in language of remarkable power, precision and beauty. Glossary of archaic terms. 80pp. 5³⁄₁₆ x 8¼. 26686-9

THE BATTLES THAT CHANGED HISTORY, Fletcher Pratt. Eminent historian profiles 16 crucial conflicts, ancient to modern, that changed the course of civilization. 352pp. 5⅜ x 8½. 41129-X

THE WIT AND HUMOR OF OSCAR WILDE, Alvin Redman (ed.). More than 1,000 ripostes, paradoxes, wisecracks: Work is the curse of the drinking classes; I can resist everything except temptation; etc. 258pp. 5⅜ x 8½.   20602-5

SHAKESPEARE LEXICON AND QUOTATION DICTIONARY, Alexander Schmidt. Full definitions, locations, shades of meaning in every word in plays and poems. More than 50,000 exact quotations. 1,485pp. 6½ x 9¼. 2-vol. set.
Vol. 1: 22726-X
Vol. 2: 22727-8

SELECTED POEMS, Emily Dickinson. Over 100 best-known, best-loved poems by one of America's foremost poets, reprinted from authoritative early editions. No comparable edition at this price. Index of first lines. 64pp. 5³⁄₁₆ x 8¼.   26466-1

THE INSIDIOUS DR. FU-MANCHU, Sax Rohmer. The first of the popular mystery series introduces a pair of English detectives to their archnemesis, the diabolical Dr. Fu-Manchu. Flavorful atmosphere, fast-paced action, and colorful characters enliven this classic of the genre. 208pp. 5³⁄₁₆ x 8¼.   29898-1

THE MALLEUS MALEFICARUM OF KRAMER AND SPRENGER, translated by Montague Summers. Full text of most important witchhunter's "bible," used by both Catholics and Protestants. 278pp. 6⅝ x 10.   22802-9

SPANISH STORIES/CUENTOS ESPAÑOLES: A Dual-Language Book, Angel Flores (ed.). Unique format offers 13 great stories in Spanish by Cervantes, Borges, others. Faithful English translations on facing pages. 352pp. 5⅜ x 8½.   25399-6

GARDEN CITY, LONG ISLAND, IN EARLY PHOTOGRAPHS, 1869–1919, Mildred H. Smith. Handsome treasury of 118 vintage pictures, accompanied by carefully researched captions, document the Garden City Hotel fire (1899), the Vanderbilt Cup Race (1908), the first airmail flight departing from the Nassau Boulevard Aerodrome (1911), and much more. 96pp. 8⅞ x 11¾.   40669-5

OLD QUEENS, N.Y., IN EARLY PHOTOGRAPHS, Vincent F. Seyfried and William Asadorian. Over 160 rare photographs of Maspeth, Jamaica, Jackson Heights, and other areas. Vintage views of DeWitt Clinton mansion, 1939 World's Fair and more. Captions. 192pp. 8⅞ x 11.   26358-4

CAPTURED BY THE INDIANS: 15 Firsthand Accounts, 1750-1870, Frederick Drimmer. Astounding true historical accounts of grisly torture, bloody conflicts, relentless pursuits, miraculous escapes and more, by people who lived to tell the tale. 384pp. 5⅜ x 8½.   24901-8

THE WORLD'S GREAT SPEECHES (Fourth Enlarged Edition), Lewis Copeland, Lawrence W. Lamm, and Stephen J. McKenna. Nearly 300 speeches provide public speakers with a wealth of updated quotes and inspiration–from Pericles' funeral oration and William Jennings Bryan's "Cross of Gold Speech" to Malcolm X's powerful words on the Black Revolution and Earl of Spenser's tribute to his sister, Diana, Princess of Wales. 944pp. 5⅜ x 8⅜.   40903-1

THE BOOK OF THE SWORD, Sir Richard F. Burton. Great Victorian scholar/adventurer's eloquent, erudite history of the "queen of weapons"–from prehistory to early Roman Empire. Evolution and development of early swords, variations (sabre, broadsword, cutlass, scimitar, etc.), much more. 336pp. 6⅛ x 9¼.
25434-8

AUTOBIOGRAPHY: The Story of My Experiments with Truth, Mohandas K. Gandhi. Boyhood, legal studies, purification, the growth of the Satyagraha (nonviolent protest) movement. Critical, inspiring work of the man responsible for the freedom of India. 480pp. 5⅜ x 8½. (Available in U.S. only.) 24593-4

CELTIC MYTHS AND LEGENDS, T. W. Rolleston. Masterful retelling of Irish and Welsh stories and tales. Cuchulain, King Arthur, Deirdre, the Grail, many more. First paperback edition. 58 full-page illustrations. 512pp. 5⅜ x 8½. 26507-2

THE PRINCIPLES OF PSYCHOLOGY, William James. Famous long course complete, unabridged. Stream of thought, time perception, memory, experimental methods; great work decades ahead of its time. 94 figures. 1,391pp. 5⅜ x 8½. 2-vol. set.
Vol. I: 20381-6 Vol. II: 20382-4

THE WORLD AS WILL AND REPRESENTATION, Arthur Schopenhauer. Definitive English translation of Schopenhauer's life work, correcting more than 1,000 errors, omissions in earlier translations. Translated by E. F. J. Payne. Total of 1,269pp. 5⅜ x 8½. 2-vol. set. Vol. 1: 21761-2 Vol. 2: 21762-0

MAGIC AND MYSTERY IN TIBET, Madame Alexandra David-Neel. Experiences among lamas, magicians, sages, sorcerers, Bonpa wizards. A true psychic discovery. 32 illustrations. 321pp. 5⅜ x 8½. (Available in U.S. only.) 22682-4

THE EGYPTIAN BOOK OF THE DEAD, E. A. Wallis Budge. Complete reproduction of Ani's papyrus, finest ever found. Full hieroglyphic text, interlinear transliteration, word-for-word translation, smooth translation. 533pp. 6½ x 9¼. 21866-X

MATHEMATICS FOR THE NONMATHEMATICIAN, Morris Kline. Detailed, college-level treatment of mathematics in cultural and historical context, with numerous exercises. Recommended Reading Lists. Tables. Numerous figures. 641pp. 5⅜ x 8½.
24823-2

PROBABILISTIC METHODS IN THE THEORY OF STRUCTURES, Isaac Elishakoff. Well-written introduction covers the elements of the theory of probability from two or more random variables, the reliability of such multivariable structures, the theory of random function, Monte Carlo methods of treating problems incapable of exact solution, and more. Examples. 502pp. 5⅜ x 8½. 40691-1

THE RIME OF THE ANCIENT MARINER, Gustave Doré, S. T. Coleridge. Doré's finest work; 34 plates capture moods, subtleties of poem. Flawless full-size reproductions printed on facing pages with authoritative text of poem. "Beautiful. Simply beautiful."–*Publisher's Weekly.* 77pp. 9¼ x 12. 22305-1

NORTH AMERICAN INDIAN DESIGNS FOR ARTISTS AND CRAFTSPEOPLE, Eva Wilson. Over 360 authentic copyright-free designs adapted from Navajo blankets, Hopi pottery, Sioux buffalo hides, more. Geometrics, symbolic figures, plant and animal motifs, etc. 128pp. 8⅜ x 11. (Not for sale in the United Kingdom.) 25341-4

SCULPTURE: Principles and Practice, Louis Slobodkin. Step-by-step approach to clay, plaster, metals, stone; classical and modern. 253 drawings, photos. 255pp. 8⅛ x 11.
22960-2

THE INFLUENCE OF SEA POWER UPON HISTORY, 1660–1783, A. T. Mahan. Influential classic of naval history and tactics still used as text in war colleges. First paperback edition. 4 maps. 24 battle plans. 640pp. 5⅜ x 8½. 25509-3

CATALOG OF DOVER BOOKS

THE STORY OF THE TITANIC AS TOLD BY ITS SURVIVORS, Jack Winocour (ed.). What it was really like. Panic, despair, shocking inefficiency, and a little heroism. More thrilling than any fictional account. 26 illustrations. 320pp. 5⅜ x 8½. 20610-6

FAIRY AND FOLK TALES OF THE IRISH PEASANTRY, William Butler Yeats (ed.). Treasury of 64 tales from the twilight world of Celtic myth and legend: "The Soul Cages," "The Kildare Pooka," "King O'Toole and his Goose," many more. Introduction and Notes by W. B. Yeats. 352pp. 5⅜ x 8½. 26941-8

BUDDHIST MAHAYANA TEXTS, E. B. Cowell and others (eds.). Superb, accurate translations of basic documents in Mahayana Buddhism, highly important in history of religions. The Buddha-karita of Asvaghosha, Larger Sukhavativyuha, more. 448pp. 5⅜ x 8½. 25552-2

ONE TWO THREE . . . INFINITY: Facts and Speculations of Science, George Gamow. Great physicist's fascinating, readable overview of contemporary science: number theory, relativity, fourth dimension, entropy, genes, atomic structure, much more. 128 illustrations. Index. 352pp. 5⅜ x 8½. 25664-2

EXPERIMENTATION AND MEASUREMENT, W. J. Youden. Introductory manual explains laws of measurement in simple terms and offers tips for achieving accuracy and minimizing errors. Mathematics of measurement, use of instruments, experimenting with machines. 1994 edition. Foreword. Preface. Introduction. Epilogue. Selected Readings. Glossary. Index. Tables and figures. 128pp. 5⅜ x 8½. 40451-X

DALÍ ON MODERN ART: The Cuckolds of Antiquated Modern Art, Salvador Dalí. Influential painter skewers modern art and its practitioners. Outrageous evaluations of Picasso, Cézanne, Turner, more. 15 renderings of paintings discussed. 44 calligraphic decorations by Dalí. 96pp. 5⅜ x 8½. (Available in U.S. only.) 29220-7

ANTIQUE PLAYING CARDS: A Pictorial History, Henry René D'Allemagne. Over 900 elaborate, decorative images from rare playing cards (14th–20th centuries): Bacchus, death, dancing dogs, hunting scenes, royal coats of arms, players cheating, much more. 96pp. 9¼ x 12¼. 29265-7

MAKING FURNITURE MASTERPIECES: 30 Projects with Measured Drawings, Franklin H. Gottshall. Step-by-step instructions, illustrations for constructing handsome, useful pieces, among them a Sheraton desk, Chippendale chair, Spanish desk, Queen Anne table and a William and Mary dressing mirror. 224pp. 8⅛ x 11¼. 29338-6

THE FOSSIL BOOK: A Record of Prehistoric Life, Patricia V. Rich et al. Profusely illustrated definitive guide covers everything from single-celled organisms and dinosaurs to birds and mammals and the interplay between climate and man. Over 1,500 illustrations. 760pp. 7½ x 10⅛. 29371-8

Paperbound unless otherwise indicated. Available at your book dealer, online at **www.doverpublications.com**, or by writing to Dept. GI, Dover Publications, Inc., 31 East 2nd Street, Mineola, NY 11501. For current price information or for free catalogues (please indicate field of interest), write to Dover Publications or log on to **www.doverpublications.com** and see every Dover book in print. Dover publishes more than 500 books each year on science, elementary and advanced mathematics, biology, music, art, literary history, social sciences, and other areas.